THE LAZY ENVIRONMENTALIST ON A BUDGET

The Lazy Environment-alist on a Budget

Save Money.
Save Time. Save the Planet.

Josh Dorfman

Stewart, Tabori & Chang
NEW YORK

Published in 2009 by Stewart, Tabori & Chang
An imprint of Harry N. Abrams, Inc.

Text copyright © 2009 by Josh Dorfman

Library of Congress Cataloging-in-Publication Data:

Dorfman, Josh.
    The lazy environmentalist on a budget : save money, save time, save the planet / by Josh Dorfman.
        p. cm.
    ISBN 978-1-58479-751-7
    1. Environmental protection—Citizen participation. 2. Environmentalism. 3. Organic living. 4. Sustainable living. I. Title.
    TD171.7.D672 2009
    640—dc26
                        2008044895

Editor: Dervla Kelly
Designer: Pamela Geismar
Production Manager: Tina Cameron

The text of this book was composed in Perpetua and Rotis Sans.

The Lazy Environmentalist was printed on Rolland Enviro 100 made with 100% post-consumer waste and processed chlorine free. Rolland Enviro 100 is certified Ecologo and FSC Recycled, and manufactured using BioGas energy.

Printed and bound in the United States of America

10 9 8 7 6 5 4 3 2 1

HNA ■■■■■
harry n. abrams, inc.
a subsidiary of La Martinière Groupe
115 West 18th Street
New York, NY 10011
www.hnabooks.com

CONTENTS

In 2007, I wrote my first book, *The Lazy Environmentalist: Your Guide to Easy, Stylish, Green Living*, which informed readers about eco-innovation that makes green living not just possible, but enjoyable. The book avoided environmental guilt trips and allusions to gloom and doom—I've found that those tactics are ineffective at motivating people to participate in long-term change. I'm much more excited about inspiring people to create significant environmental change by presenting solutions that are easy and stylish and clearly in their self-interest. That's what I set out to do with *The Lazy Environmentalist*. By introducing an array of products and services that not only improve the health of the planet but also vastly improve the quality of our lives, I hoped that readers would discover that it's awesome to go green.

Once the book was published, I received lots of positive feedback. People were hungry for the solutions presented in its pages and relieved to be free from the guilt or hopelessness that frequently accompanies a book written by an environmentalist. I was proud to be reaching so many people with this message of possibility and to be offering hundreds of choices for leading a stylish green lifestyle. But there was just one problem: Very few people were taking my advice—often readers were not implementing the ideas I had outlined. I wanted to know why.

It didn't take long to find the answer. Voicing these frustrations to my brother over beers one Sunday afternoon, he set me straight. "Dude, I don't know where to get green products. If I did, I wouldn't know which ones are good and which ones stink. And if I found the good ones, how could I be sure that they were actually better for the planet than what I'm using today? But really, dude, it's all too expensive to bother with in the first place."

So, to my brother and everyone else who wants to live an *affordable* green life, I present *The Lazy Environmentalist on a Budget*, a guide to environmental choices that are easy, affordable, readily accessible, and better for the planet than conventional options available today. Will a $15 low-flow showerhead solve our planet's problems? I don't know. But I do know that it will help you by lowering your heating and water bills and will help the planet by saving thousands of gallons of water each year (as well as the fossil-fuel energy required to make that water hot). With that showerhead's multiple spray options, you'll also discover that helping the planet can be a refreshing and enjoyable experience (see Chapter 5: Eco-H2O).

The solutions you'll read about in this book don't require much effort or financial commitment, yet their eco-significance is as great (sometimes greater) than those requiring big money and big struggle. For example, did you know that recycling your computer and other electronics can be easy *and* profitable? That's the deal at Myboneyard.com, a company that will recycle your electronics and cut you a check based on their residual value. Or that you can update your wardrobe without spending any money? Say hello to Swapstyle.com, a website that lets you trade clothing with fashionistas across the globe. And what about opting out of our mass consumer society by renting the things you need—like blowtorches, juicers, and golf clubs—instead of buying the gear and using it once? Irent2u.com has the answer (see Chapter 1: The 3Rs).

Our ability to go green simply, affordably, and with supreme style is also getting a boost from the world's largest corporations. Whether shopping for outdoor furniture, organic bedding, or baby products, Wal-Mart offers eco-options at rock bottom prices (see Chapter 7: Eco at Home and Chapter 9: Better for Baby). Clorox is responding to consumer demand for healthy home-cleaning products through Green Works, its highly regarded line of plant-based, natural cleaners (see Chapter 8: A Greener Way to Clean). And Brita is raising awareness about the environmental degradation caused by billions of used disposable water bottles through its FilterForGood.com campaign (see Chapter 1:The 3Rs). I've been so impressed with the ways in which these companies are helping consumers make easy and affordable environmental choices that I've chosen to collaborate with them in media outreach and, in some instances, as a spokesperson. You can learn more about their green consumer initiatives and those of other major brands and companies in the pages that follow.

Often I'm asked about where this green living trend is heading. To me, it seems inevitable that our lifestyles and more broadly our global economy will one day function in balance with nature's capabilities to sustain it. Yet, *how soon* that day arrives is really the key question to consider. While we already possess the know-how to solve global warming and other looming environmental challenges, what we don't possess is unlimited time to implement the solutions. *The Lazy Environmentalist on a Budget* will help you make the decisions that will shift your lifestyle into balance with nature. The sooner we do so, the sooner we'll create the change in the world that we want to see.

1

The Three Rs

Reduce
Reuse &
Recycle

The 3 Rs (Reduce, Reuse, and Recycle) is no longer simply a mantra for environmental activists, it's a ticket to saving you money while you consider the planet. The 3Rs ask you to buy less, reuse more, and recycle products at the end of their useful life—wonderful guiding principles for reducing our environmental footprint and bringing our lifestyles into balance with nature. But in practice, how many of us are really willing to cut back on the stuff we want to own, to reuse what we'd like to throw out, and to recycle when doing so is often incredibly inconvenient?

Fortunately for budget-conscious Lazy Environmentalists, the 3Rs are receiving a twenty-first-century facelift, making them easy to implement and even easier on the wallet. We have entered a moment when we no longer have to invest in our own gear (be it a chainsaw, pasta maker, or Ping Pong table); we don't have to hit the mall to refresh our wardrobe; and we don't have to hunt for the recycling drop-off point to keep our used cell phones (or computers or stereo speakers) out of the landfill. The 3Rs are easier than ever to embrace, and doing so can help you maintain your lifestyle while saving you money. This first chapter will introduce you to eco-aware products and services that support the 3R mission and that will be covered in greater detail throughout the book.

REDUCE

Reduce, the first of the 3Rs, releases you from the hassle, expense, and waste of unwanted stuff while helping you use less energy and create less trash. And while most of us can't imagine life without our most prized four-wheeled possession, the first place to embrace Reduce is with our cars. That's because our automobiles generate about half of our personal greenhouse gas emissions—the other half comes from our homes.

Today, you can enjoy the freedom of being in the driver's seat while eliminating all of the expense of owning—or leasing—and maintaining a car by joining a car-share service. Zipcar is leading the way. Available in more than 40 U.S. cities, Zipcar lets members locate cars conveniently parked at designated spots around the city and reserve them for an hourly fee (typically between $10.50 and $16.50). Members arrive at the parking spot, swipe their membership card over the windshield sensor to unlock the door, hop in, and go. There's no need to pay for gasoline or insurance; Zipcar has got you covered. You won't sacrifice your ride either; Zipcar lets you choose from models like the BMW 325, Mini Cooper, Honda Fit, Volkswagen Jetta, Toyota Prius, Honda Civic Hybrid, Volvo S40, Mazda 3, and Subaru Outback. According to the company's surveys, over time Zipcar members reduce their car usage by as much as 50 percent. They always have access to cars, but also become more inclined to walk, bike, take public transit, or hop in a taxi (it's okay, you won't go to hell for taking a taxi). As for the reduction in greenhouse gas emissions and traffic congestion, Zipcar estimates that each of its cars removes the equivalent of about 15 privately owned vehicles from the road.

Other car-sharing services are popping up across the country. Check out CommunityCar.com when you're in Madison, Wisconsin; HourCar.org when visiting Minneapolis, Minnesota; and PhillyCarShare.org when hanging in Philadelphia, Pennsylvania. Car-sharing is proving so popular with people who appreciate the convenience of having a car constantly accessible—without having to ask Mom or Dad for permission to use it—that Enterprise Rent-A-Car, the largest rental car company in the world, has started WeCar, a car-share service currently available in St. Louis, Missouri.

Car-sharing is largely for city dwellers, but suburbanites can reduce their gasoline consumption and car ownership too with ride sharing, i.e., carpooling. Several companies have discovered how to make sharing a ride easy, fun, and even rewarding. In fact, these days whether you're looking for a ride to work, soccer practice, or a rock concert, services like Zimride, NuRide, and GoLoco.org ensure that there's a very good chance somebody else is going your way (see a full discussion in Chapter 3: Tread Lightly).

Reducing your eco-impact by consuming less stuff is pretty much Environmentalism 101. That's because making new consumer products—be it T-shirts or baseball gloves or TVs—has an ecological impact. A lot of energy and water is needed to grow or extract raw materials from the earth, and the same is true for turning those raw materials into new products. But it's now possible to consume fewer products and still get exactly what we want. Sound paradoxical? Not if you're perusing the inventory available at Irent2u.com. The website lets you rent products from neighbors or anyone else nearby who is willing to make their own stuff available (and make a few bucks in the process). Instead of purchasing that John Deere lawn tractor only to use it a handful of times, you can rent it for a fraction of the retail price. Need to bone up on your Italian before your next vacation? Rent some language tapes. Want to try golf? Rent some golf clubs. The possibilities are limitless. And if you'd like to earn a little extra cash, list some of your own items for rent. Similar services are popping up across the globe. Check out Zilok.com in France, Germany's eRento, and New Zealand's Hirethings.co.nz.

Heading off to college soon and nervous about the spiraling costs of textbooks? Chegg.com has the answer. The company rents more than a million textbook titles, helping students save up to 80 percent off retail prices and potentially hundreds of dollars each semester. The company also plants one tree for every textbook it rents. Once the semester is over, print out a pre-paid mailing label provided by Chegg.com and send the books back to the company, so next semester's students can also expand their minds and reduce their eco-footprints.

You can also apply the concept of Reducing to decrease the amount of waste you generate. Start your new "waste-loss" regime with a water filtration system that lets you enjoy endless amounts of tasty tap water while eliminating unwanted substances—lead, chlorine, copper, and mercury to name a few—that could be in your water. And you'll save money as you wean yourself off your disposable water bottle habit—a practice that collectively results in more than 38 billion disposable plastic bottles deposited in the landfill each year in the United States. The easy affordable filter of choice is a Brita pitcher. Simply pour tap water through the top of the pitcher and it will drain through the replaceable filter (made primarily of reclaimed coconut husks), and presto, you're ready to drink. Sleek space-saving models like the Brita Slim ($10.99) can hold up to 40 ounces and are narrow enough to fit on the shelf of a refrigerator door. The Brita Deluxe ($26.99) is a larger, elegantly designed model that holds up to 80 ounces of water. Each pitcher filter ($24.99 for a 3-pack) delivers the same amount of fresh drinking water as about 300 standard 16.9-ounce bottles. That's why drinking from your Brita is one of the easiest ways to save money and reduce waste. And when your replaceable pitcher filter is used up, recycle it. Early in 2009, Brita launched a new program with eco-products maker Preserve to recycle the plastic from used filters into a sleek line of personal care, tableware, and kitchen-ware products. You can drop off filters at participating Whole Foods Markets or mail them directly to Preserve.

This Lazy Environmentalist is a huge fan of Brita, which is why I've signed on as a spokesperson for Brita's FilterForGood campaign. The campaign invites you to take the pledge to give up disposable bottled water for a week, month, or year. To help you reach your goal it also offers reusable FilterForGood water bottles courtesy of Nalgene. The sporty and classic plastic bottles sell for $10 and are BPA-free (a questionable chemical that is believed to adversely harm the human body). Visit Filterforgood.com to learn more.

Brita also offers water filtration systems that connect directly to your faucet or refrigerator. As for other reusable water bottles, check out Sigg's fun-filled designs that are also durable, dishwasher-safe, and nontoxic. Kleen Kanteen is another safe option for trans-porting water. The sleek stainless steel reusable bottles come in a

Pankaj Shah is founder and CEO of Green Dimes, a company that helps consumers eliminate junk mail.

How did you get the idea for Green Dimes?
The concept was an experiment. I was trying to figure out if capitalism and social good could coexist. The beauty of what we're doing is that we give consumers something they want/need and we take care of the goodness. So we're chasing lifestyle dollars, not charity dollars. I just looked at all the junk mail I received at home and started digging into how to stop it all. I thought, hey, if I care about this but don't want to spend a bunch of time getting off lists, I'd pay a nominal fee for someone else to do the work and maybe others would too.

What is Green Dimes's positive environmental impact?
Well, I think it's on two fronts. First, we plant trees for every new member that chooses a paid service. Second, because there are 100 million trees and 28 billion gallons of water used each year to produce unsolicited mail, every time someone signs up for Green Dimes we're able to help reduce those numbers.

I hear it's hard to get off Victoria's Secret's catalog list. How many people would you say are really upset about this?
Not enough! Though you might be surprised to know that Victoria's Secret is by far our number one opt-out request, and they're the hardest company to work with.

variety of colors. Platypus reusable bottles are made of BPA-free plastic and can be stored flat inside your backpack or handbag when not in use. And Pure Water 2Go reusable bottles are equipped with their own built-in filtration system, giving you freedom to roam where the skies are vast and the water is stale.

Waste can be really devious, collecting in big piles in your mailbox or on your doorstep before you know what has happened. This phenomenon is called "junk mail," and most of us have to contend with lots of it—about 100 pounds per year for the average U.S. household. Don't get bogged down under heaps of catalogs and credit card promotions. Instead let a company called Green Dimes remove your name from consumer mailing lists and reduce the clutter from your life. For a one-time fee of $20, your name will be removed from more than 90 percent of all junk mail lists. Monthly monitoring by Green Dimes will keep you off those lists for five years. The company will even counterbalance the ill effects of your history with junk mail by planting five trees in your honor. You can also opt for Green Dimes's latest promotion package—the company will pay you to use its tools to remove yourself from junk mail lists. The first five million people who sign up for self-service will each receive $1. Since launching in 2006, Green Dimes has helped liberate hundreds of thousands of people from junk mail. Now it's your turn to experience the freedom.

REUSE

Reuse—the middle child of the 3Rs—has been a part of our lives before we were "eco" anything (eco-conscious, eco-savvy, even a tentative eco-curious). Think about it: Every day, we reuse items like T-shirts, cereal bowls, and underwear without a second thought. We don't toss them after one use. We reuse. The secret to twenty-first-century Reusing is to discover how to reuse other people's really cool stuff as well as our own; it's about learning how to let go of clutter so other people can benefit from what we've got; and it's about finding appealing ways to extend the life of products that we might otherwise dump in the trash. Similar in many ways to the first R (Reduce), Reuse allows us to tread lighter on the planet while still surrounding ourselves with goods that we enjoy.

Let's start with your jeans, perhaps the staple of any American's wardrobe. Distressed styles are still the rage these days, but when distressed turns to ratty and tattered, hope is not lost for your favorite pair of denim. Instead of tossing them in the trash and shopping for a new pair, mail them to Denim Therapy at its repair facility in Cincinnati, Ohio. Upon arrival, a denim therapist will examine holes and rips and evaluate your jeans' unique thread weight, fade, wash, pattern, weave, and wear. Your jeans will then be reconstructed and restored to their original look and feel and shipped back to you. The process takes about two to three weeks and costs $7 per inch of repair plus $12 for shipping. So go ahead, let your jeans get into a tussle or two. With Denim Therapy in your corner, even seemingly insurmountable wounds can always be healed.

But suppose you're absolutely craving a new pair of denim. You're ready to shop, but before you head to the mall to spend big bucks on new duds, try logging onto Swapstyle.com, a global community of fashionistas who trade, buy, and sell used items from their own wardrobes in exchange for the opportunity to pluck sweet finds from yours. Tired of your Hudson Jeans? Swap them for a pair of J Brand Dark Vintage. Had enough of Marc Jacobs for the moment? Swap your goods for an influx of Prada. The possibilities are limitless as you connect with members around the United States and in fashion capitals like London, Milan, and Sydney. Swapping is free. All you pay is the price of shipping. There are also no fees charged by Swapstyle.com for buying or selling. Remember, manufacturing new consumer products, even clothing and accessories, has an ecological impact. It takes lots of energy and water to grow materials like cotton or extract raw materials like oil (from which fabrics like nylon and polyester are made). The same is true for turning those raw materials into new products. Through sites like Swapstyle.com, avoiding purchasing new products is not only easy, but also a money-saving pleasure.

The same Reuse logic is in effect at Goozex.com, where gamers gather to swap their video games. While Swapstyle.com asks you to peruse the offerings of other members (at your leisure, of course), Goozex makes instantaneous matches for you. All you do is create an account and list the games you own that you'd like to trade. Then Goozex quickly locates other gamers who want them. With each game you mail, you earn Goozex points, which you can then use to acquire the games you want from other members.

Instead of spending lots of money on new games, you'll pay Goozex $1 each time you receive a game. Whether you're partial to Xbox, Wii, Nintendo, or many other gaming platforms, the Goozex trading community has got you covered. Get your reused copy of Call of Duty 2 or NCAA Football 09 today.

Swapping websites are emerging in all kinds of categories. Bookworms can browse more than two million titles available for trade at Paperbackswap.com. Movie collectors can visit Swapadvd. com to trade both new and classic DVD titles. CD fans (you know you've still got 'em) can tap into more than 130,000 titles available at Swapacd.com. And new and expecting parents can trade for baby strollers, bibs, bedding, bumpers, and more at Zwaggle.com.

Reuse may be in its finest form on The Freecycle Network (Freecycle.org). The concept is so simple you'll be surprised you didn't think of it first. Freecycle members join a local email group where they list used items that they no longer need and are willing to give away for free, or "gift," as founder Deron Beal calls it. Local members who need or want the items—like couches, cabinets, coffee tables, or Cuisinarts—arrange to pick them up. That's all there is to it. Yet this simple idea has led to an explosion of activity. Since launching in 2003, Freecycle has spread to more than 80 countries and grown to more than 5.5 million members worldwide, with 20,000 more joining every week. Members are participating in what Beal calls the global gifting economy, which collectively redirects thousands of tons of usable items away from the landfill and into the hands of those who will benefit from them.

Naturally, there are times when reusing somebody else's unwanted merchandise won't meet your needs, and buying a new product seems like the only course of action. But before you pay top dollar to consume new or invest the time to find a deal by scanning numerous shopping sites, consider looking into products that have been refurbished. This is an eco-savvy way to strike deals, particularly for items like computers, TVs, cell phones, and other electronics. Refurbished items are usually products that were returned to stores within 30 days of purchase, had damaged packaging or a slight cosmetic defect, were used as in-store display items, or were simply overstocked. Many are still covered by their original warranties. And before they can be resold in the marketplace they go through rigorous defect testing. They also frequently sell for less than 50 percent of the retail price. Taking advantage of these bargains helps keep these products out of landfills, which is where they typically end up. So, if you're looking for a megadeal on computers and other office electronics visit Refurbdepot.com. If it's an LCD or plasma flat-panel TV you want then check out Secondact.com. And for amazing deals on iPods and Blackberries head over to Dyscern. com. Yes, you can have your gadgets and your planet too.

Lastly, any discussion of Reuse would be incomplete without mentioning the paper versus plastic conundrum. Paper bags come from trees. Plastic bags come from oil. Neither choice is a productive use of the planet's natural resources. As many Lazy Environmentalists already know, the best approach is to tote your own reusable shopping bags and avoid the controversy altogether. Well and good in theory, but it's difficult to get excited about reusable, beige-colored canvas bags bearing proud slogans like "I'm an Earth Momma" or utopian slogans like "Make Love Not Carbon" or even absurdly obvious one like "This Is Not a Plastic Bag." To really accelerate the shift to shopping bag Reuse, it's helpful to add a dash of updated attitude to your canvas bag or ditch it altogether for more color and style. For a bit of attitude with your canvas bag, check out the sack from Angry Little Girls featuring a cartoon of one little girl admonishing another to "Shop with a reusable bag, B*tch!" And for a bag with supreme color and style, check out Envirosax's collections. The contemporary Mikado line from the Graphic Series is inspired by ornate Japanese motifs and features bold floral graphics and intricate geometrical patterns. With shagadelic circles and interlocking rectangles, the Retro Graphic Line is an homage to seventies chic. Prices for these lightweight, waterproof bags start at $8.50. There are five bags in each line and a complete set (all five) with accompanying stowing pouch can be purchased for $37.95. The only downside is that they're made from polyester, a plastic derived from oil. Recognizing the concern among consumers, however, Envirosax has also introduced its Organic Series of stylish reusable bags made from natural, eco-friendly fabrics such as bamboo, hemp, and linen. The patterns are equally fabulous, though beige reigns supreme as the dominant color. Prices also leap to $24.95 per bag, a little on the steep side but perhaps not too shabby for a tote that walks the walk while turning heads at the farmers' market.

RECYCLE

Recycle, the last of the 3R trio, is the most transformative of the Rs. When we recycle, we're giving used products the chance to be reborn as something new. In the coming chapters, you'll discover innovative companies that are finding ways to turn recycled materials into an array of affordable and exceptional green products. There's Preserve, a company based in Waltham, Massachusetts, that has partnered with Stonyfield Farm to recycle its yogurt cups—from organic yogurt, of course—into ergonomic plastic toothbrushes, razors, and an assortment of colorful kitchenware (and now does the same with Brita pitcher filters). TerraCycle, based in Trenton, New Jersey, is on pace to redefine much of America's relationship with trash. The company that began with its signature Plant Food—made from worm poop, packaged in empty Pepsi bottles and sold at the likes of Home Depot and Wal-Mart—has evolved into an innovation powerhouse that continually introduces new products made entirely from waste. Take the E-Water Trash Cans and Recycling Bins available at OfficeMax for $10.99 each and made from crushed computers and fax machines (that would otherwise end up in a landfill). Or the rain barrels and composters made from Kendall-Jackson oak wine barrels that sell for $99 each at Sam's Club. They're both prime examples of a company that sees opportunity where others see garbage. In 2008, TerraCycle announced a major partnership with Kraft Foods to take used packaging from brands like Oreo cookies, Chips Ahoy!, Balance bars, South Beach Living bars, and Capri Sun beverages and transform them into attractive consumer products. Cookie wrappers will soon be fused into sheets of water-proof fabric and then transformed into umbrellas, shower curtains, backpacks, place mats, and more. Energy bar wrappers will make backpacks and purses. Drink pouches are already being given new life in a wide assortment of bags, including funky totes ($7.99 to $11.99), messenger bags ($19.99), backpacks ($11.99), and lunch-boxes ($7.99). How does TerraCycle get its hands on so much garbage? By signing up trash collecting "brigades" across the United States. Thousands of schools, nonprofit organizations, and business offices are collecting waste and sending it to TerraCycle's facility. In exchange, the schools and nonprofits gain an additional income

Interview

Ron Gonen is co-founder and CEO of RecycleBank, a company that makes recycling easy, understandable, and rewarding.

How did you get the idea for RecycleBank?
I always had an interest in social policy and the environment. New York City cut back its recycling in 2002, and it gave us the idea to find a way to make recycling work.

What is RecycleBank's positive environmental impact?
Recycling saves trees and oil (plastic is made from petroleum). I think our biggest environmental impact is helping people understand the economic value of being green.

What's the most valuable material your company recycles? The most dangerous? Worst smelling?
Cardboard is the most valuable, and e-waste (electronics) is the most dangerous. Nothing smells sweeter to me than a RecycleBank cart full of recyclables.

stream or opt (as do offices) to donate proceeds to a local charity of their choosing.

While exciting young companies are capitalizing on recycling, the third R enables you to profit too. Start with your electronics. To prevent the dumping of electronic items in landfills—an enormous environmental challenge called "E-Waste"—companies like Dell, IBM, HP, and Apple will take used computers and electronics back free of charge. But you invested in your gear and deserve more than "free of charge" when it's time to give it up—you deserve to get paid! That's where MyBoneyard.com comes in. Simple drop-down menus inform visitors of the residual market value of their desktop computers, laptops, and monitors, and cell phones. MyBoneyard.com then provides users with a prepaid printable shipping label. Once you mail your products back to the company and their condition is verified, MyBoneyard.com will mail you a check. It's that simple.

A similar Recycle philosophy fuels GreenPhone.com. The site tells you how much your cell phone or PDA model is worth and then allows you to mail it in for cash. The Environmental Protection Agency (EPA) estimates that across the United States, more than 500 million old cell phones languish in desk drawers and other storage spots. Disposing of these devices properly is of vital environmental concern since they contain hazardous chemicals like arsenic and lead that can be released into the atmosphere, soil, and groundwater. GreenPhone.com allows you to protect the environment while earning a little spending money—never a bad thing. And if you're feeling more virtuous, visit GreenPhone.com's sister site, CollectiveGood.com, which offers the same service and donates your proceeds to charity.

What about plastic, paper, glass, cardboard, and aluminum, the stuff of everyday recycling? Unfortunately, recycling these basics is not always easy and rarely profitable. Enter RecycleBank. Residents in participating communities receive a large RecycleBank garbage bin for all of their recyclables. No need to sort, just toss it all in. The bin is embedded with a barcode that doubles as your account number. When the recycling truck comes to collect your garbage, it reads the barcode and scans the bin for weight and volume to get a sense of what's inside. The recyclables then go on to a recycling center. When you log in at RecycleBank.com with your account number, you'll see how much you've earned from recycling. You can then redeem that value at more than 300 RecycleBank retail partners, like Bed, Bath & Beyond, CVS, Petco, Circuit City, and Amazon.com. The benefits of the program really start to add up: You earn money by recycling, your city saves taxpayer money from reduced landfill fees, the environment gets cleaner as recyclable products actually get recycled, and the local economy gets a boost from new jobs created at local recycling centers. Welcome to the new economics of modern Recycling: better for your budget, better for the community, and better for the planet.

Reduce Products and Services

BRITA
Brita.com
A Brita water filtration system is an affordable, convenient way to get great tasting water while reducing disposable water bottle waste. The simplest way to get started is with a Brita pitcher. The Brita Slim is one of 11 available models and starts at just $10.99 and can hold up to 40 ounces of water. Faucet mount and refrigerator water filtration systems are also available.

CHEGG
Chegg.com
Chegg rents more than a million textbook titles, helping students save up to 80 percent off retail prices and potentially hundreds of dollars each semester while reducing the need to cut down trees to make new textbooks. The company also plants one tree for every textbook it rents.

GOLOCO.ORG
Share rides to work, concerts, sporting events, or even the farmers' market using GoLoco. The company's website utilizes Facebook's social networking platform, enabling users to create personal profiles and choose compatible riding companions. The website also handles all financial transactions to remove the awkwardness of requesting gas and toll money from fellow travelers.

GREEN DIMES

Greendimes.com

Green Dimes is helping consumers eliminate 90 percent of unwanted junk mail for up to five years at a time. When you sign up for the service, Green Dimes removes your name from all mailing lists that you don't want to be on but keeps you on the ones you do, thereby saving trees, carbon emissions from transportation, and the hassle of having to recycle all that junk.

HULU

Hulu.com

Watch your favorite TV shows for free at Hulu.com. Check out current and past episodes of *The Office, It's Always Sunny in Philadelphia, Arrested Development, Family Guy, House*, and many more. Free movies are available too. Commercial interruptions are limited, and the viewing experience is excellent. How is it possible? At Hulu.com, the major networks have come together to make their content available in one location. They're betting that if it's all in one place they'll attract enough viewers to make some money. That's all well and good, but as far as Lazy Environmentalists are concerned, Hulu.com might just reduce your need to ever buy a new TV.

IRENT2U.COM

Instead of buying new consumer products, rent what you need from others for a fraction of the price. If you'd like to earn a little extra cash, list some of your own items for rent. With Irent2u.com you can buy less and still get exactly what you want when you want it.

NEIGHBORROW

Neighborrow.com

Instead of buying or even renting items, just borrow them from your neighbor. Neighborrow.com helps facilitate the process by enabling members to list items that they're willing to loan. Whether you're looking for books, movies, music, power tools, tractors, or an egg beater, Neighborrow might have just the item for you. No money exchanges hands, and you can also trade items that you're no longer interested in keeping.

NURIDE

Nuride.com

Nuride is an online ride-sharing service with more than 28,000 members who receive reward points for sharing rides. The service operates just like an airline membership rewards program. The more rides you share, the more points you earn, and the more value you can redeem. Partners include Applebee's, Austin Grill, Dunkin' Donuts, and Ringling Brothers and Barnum & Bailey Circus.

WECAR

Wecar.com

Rental car giant Enterprise Rent-A-Car has partnered with the city of St. Louis, Missouri, to introduce its WeCar car-share service. Members can take advantage of an all-hybrid fleet of cars parked at convenient locations throughout the downtown area.

ZIMRIDE

Zimride.com

Zimride is a ride-share service built on a social networking platform, enabling members to create personal profiles and select ride mates who share similar music tastes, favorite sports teams, or who just seem "normal." Zimmers can also evaluate things like driving speed, music volume, and smoking preferences before agreeing to hop in. Find rides at Zimride.com or by using Zimride's Facebook application, which makes the service available to Facebook's 80 million users.

ZINIO

Zinio.com

Zinio takes you into the age of digital magazine subscriptions and reduces the need for all that paper. At Zinio.com you can subscribe to more than 500 titles, like *BusinessWeek, Cosmopolitan, Car & Driver, Men's Health, Dwell, Outside,* and *Yoga Journal.* Download the Zinio Reader and read the magazines on your computer or access your subscriptions online from any computer at Zinio.com. iPhone owners can even access entire magazines through their phones.

ZIPCAR

Zipcar.com

Zipcar is like, "Hey Dad, can I borrow your car tonight?" without having to ask your dad. This car-share service is perfect for people who normally use public transportation but need a vehicle for a couple of hours or a day for a doctor's appointment, beach excursion, or a night on the town. Membership is minimal and the cars are new, stylish, and available in cities all over the country.

Reuse Services

DENIM THERAPY

Denimtherapy.com

Tattered jeans can be successfully repaired and restored by Denim Therapy at its facility in Cincinnati. For $7 per inch of repair (plus $12 shipping), denim therapists will repair holes and rips and restore the look and feel of your jeans by considering the unique thread weight, fade, wash, pattern, weave, wear, and look of your go-to pair. Pop your jeans in the mail, and they'll be back to you and better than ever in just two to three weeks.

DYSCERN

Dyscern.com

For amazing deals on refurbished iPods, Blackberries, PDAs, and other cell phones, look no further than Dyscern.com. The inventory is extensive at this online retailer that specializes in the recovery and resale of products that would otherwise most likely end up in landfills.

GOOZEX

Goozex.com

Whether you're partial to Xbox, Wii, Nintendo, or other gaming platforms, the Goozex online trading community has got games for you, with 2,400 of the most advanced and feature-rich video games to choose from. Instead of spending lots of money on new games, Goozex charges you just $1 each time you receive a game from another community member.

PAPERBACKSWAP.COM

Bookworms can browse more than 2 million titles available for trade at Paperbackswap.com. Upload your own titles and send them to community members to earn credits. Use the credits to obtain books that you want. And it's not just paperbacks that are available to trade—hardcover books are on offer too.

REFURB DEPOT

Refurbdepot.com

Find tremendous deals on refurbished desktop and laptop computers, printers, scanners, copy machines, fax machines, and much more. Many items are still covered by their original warranties and frequently sold for more than 50 percent off the retail price.

SECOND ACT

Secondact.com

If it's an LCD or plasma flat-panel HDTV you want, check out Secondact. com for unbelievable deals on refurbished models. Buying refurbished models helps keep them out of landfills while reducing consumption of new consumer products. You can enjoy your big screen and do your part for the planet too.

SWAPACD.COM

CD fans can access more than 130,000 available titles at Swapacd.com. Load in your own CD titles and join the community to starting earning credits. It costs 49 cents plus one credit and shipping to obtain a CD from any other member.

SWAPADVD.COM

Movie collectors can visit Swapadvd.com to trade both new and classic DVD titles. More than 58,000 titles are available, and the number is growing as more people discover the cost benefits of swapping used DVDs.

SWAP STYLE

Swapstyle.com

Swaptstyle.com is like browsing through thousands of people's closets and picking out only the things you absolutely have to have. Swap accessories, cosmetics, and shoes with fashionistas all over the globe for free. All you pay is the price of shipping.

THE FREECYCLE NETWORK

Freecycle.org

Freecycle enables local community members to give away, or "gift," items— like couches, cabinets, coffee tables, or Cuisinarts—to others in the community who want them. Visit Freecycle.org to sign up for your local email list and start participating in what founder Deron Beal calls "the global gifting economy."

ZWAGGLE

Zwaggle.com

Swap gently used baby and children's items like strollers, baby furniture, or toys with parents throughout the United States by joining Zwaggle.com. Sign up to get your Zwaggle Points (Zoints) and use them to trade your items for the baby gear you need. The service is free aside from shipping costs, and shipping is made easy through Zwaggle's integrated FedEx tool.

Reusable Shopping Bags

ANGRY LITTLE GIRLS

Angrylittlegirls.com

For a reusable canvas shopping bag with a bit of attitude and edge, check out the site of actress and cartoonist Leila Lee. Among her many bags is one featuring a cartoon of one little girl admonishing another to "Shop with a reusable bag, B*tch!" Purchase it for $14.99.

BAGGU

Baggubag.com

Made from super-strong ripstop nylon that holds up to 25 pounds of weight, one Baggu holds the contents of 2 to 3 plastic grocery bags. The bags are brightly colored and fold into a mini-pouch for stowing. Purchase one for $8, a 3-set for $22, and a 6-set for $38. According to the company, using one Baggu for one year replaces 300 to 700 disposable bags.

CHICO

Chicobag.com

It's the ultracompact reusable nylon bag that's small enough to fit in your pocket until you're ready to bust it out to the delight of check-out clerks, fellow line-mates, and the planet. Kick the single-use habit with these $5 bags (every fifth one you purchase is free) that also feature a built-in key chain for added convenience.

ECOEZI

Ecoezi.com

Carry your machine-washable Ecoezi reusable shopping bags inside a compact, stylish Ecoezi wallet. The lightweight wallet conveniently stores 10 reusable bags (included) and is available for $21.95. Stow it in your handbag or your glove box for easy access.

ENVIROSAX

Envirosax.com

Envirosax delivers on affordability and style with its collections of reusable polyester shopping bags that make both a fashion and an environmental statement. Prices for these lightweight, waterproof bags are $8.50. Bags made from eco-fabrics such as bamboo, hemp, and linen are also available, though prices jump to $24.95 each.

FLIP & TUMBLE

Flipandtumble.com

Made of lightweight, ripstop nylon, the Flip & Tumble reusable shopping bag ($12) is heavy on durability and convenience. A padded shoulder also makes it comfortable when carrying loads up to 25 pounds. Scrunch it up into a ball and flip it into its own built-in pouch when not in use.

Reusable Water Bottles

FILTER FOR GOOD

Filterforgood.com

Pair a Brita water pitcher—for tasty filtered water—with a reusable water bottle provided by Nalgene ($10) to kick the disposable water bottle habit. At FilterForGood.com, you can sign the pledge to give up disposable water bottles and join with others around the United States who are doing the same. Check the website's interactive map to see which cities and states are leading the way.

KLEAN KANTEEN

Kleankanteen.com

Made of rugged stainless steel, Klean Kanteens ($14.95 to $25.95) are easy to clean, durable, and sanitary. Plenty of colors are available including blue, pink, orange, black, green, and tree bark (yes, tree bark is apparently a color). A slim design enables them to fit into cup holders so on-road adventurers can enjoy them as much as off-road adventurers.

PLATYPUS

Platy.com

Backpackers, travelers, and urban warriors will appreciate the lightweight Platy Bottles ($6.95 to $9.95) from Platypus that are made of BPA-free plastic and can be rolled up and stored flat inside a backpack or handbag when not in use.

PURE WATER 2GO

Purewater2go.com

Stay hydrated on the go with portable filtered water thanks to Pure Water 2Go reusable water bottles ($7.95 to $29.95) equipped with built-in filtration systems. Depending upon the model you choose, the filter will provide between 40 and 200 gallons of fresh water, giving you freedom to roam where the skies are vast and the water is stale.

SIGG

Sigg.com

Sigg reusable bottles ($16.95 to $28) come in 144 fun-filled designs and 22 interchangeable lids that make them equal parts hydration solution and fashion accessory. The nontoxic rugged aluminum bottles are leak-proof, crack-resistant, and recyclable at the end of their very long lives.

Recycle Products and Services

BUYMYTRONICS.COM

Founded by Denver-based entrepreneur Brett Mosley after his much-used and much-loved iPod broke, Buymytronics.com is on a mission to recycle used, new, and broken electronics. To make it worthwhile, the company pays you for them within 48 hours of receiving them. Send Mosley and his team your old cell phones, cameras, game consoles, camcorders, and iPods, and they'll send you cash.

CALL2RECYCLE

Call2recycle.org

Drop off dead rechargeable batteries and old cell phones at more than 30,000 Call2Recycle locations around North America. Find the bins at participating partners such as Best Buy, Office Depot, Radio Shack, Sears, and Staples. Call2Recycle either resells the products or recycles them into new batteries or other useful materials like stainless steel.

CELL PHONES FOR SOLDIERS

Cellphonesforsoldiers.com

Got an old cell phone languishing in a desk drawer or closet? Send it to Cell Phones For Soldiers and they'll make sure it ends up in the hands of a soldier overseas along with an hour of free talk time so he or she can connect with loved ones back home. About 15,000 phones are collected each month through 3,000 drop-off stations around the country. Teenagers Robbie and Brittany Bergquist started this innovative organization with $21 of their own money. Help the planet and a soldier. It won't cost you a penny.

EARTH 911

Earth911.org

Find centralized information on all things recycling by visiting Earth911 or calling its toll-free hotline at 1-800-CLEANUP. Find out how to recycle, why to recycle, and where to recycle by typing in your zip code and a specific item like compact fluorescent lightbulbs, batteries, or plastic bottles.

GREENPHONE.COM
You don't have to sell your soul to prevent global warming, but you can certainly "sell your cell." Visit Greenphone.com to find out how much your used cell phone is worth and then print the free postage label and mail your phone to the company. Once Greenphone.com receives and verifies its condition, the company will cut you a check.

MYBONEYARD
Myboneyard.com
MyBoneYard provides a simple and easy way to reduce e-waste. Instead of chucking your old Blackberry, iPod, or digital camera into the trash, visit myboneyard.com, find out how much it's still worth, mail it in, and get paid.

PRESERVE
Recycline.com
The Waltham, Massachusetts–based company has partnered with Stonyfield Farm to turn its yogurt cups—from organic yogurt, of course—into affordable and ergonomic recycled plastic toothbrushes, razors, and colorful kitchenware. Find dishwasher-safe, 100 percent recycled plastic cups, cutlery, plates, cutting boards, colanders, and storage containers. A new Preserve program with Brita now recycles the plastic from Brita pitcher filters for use in its collection too.

RECYCLEBANK
Recyclebank.com
Earn rewards for recycling your trash through RecycleBank's innovative program that lets you conveniently dump all of your recyclables into one bin. After the recycling truck collects it, log in to Recyclebank.com, enter your account number, and see how much you've earned. You can redeem that value at more than 300 RecycleBank retail partners, like Bed, Bath & Beyond, CVS, Petco, Circuit City, and Amazon.com.

SECOND ROTATION
Secondrotation.com
Send Second Rotation your used cell phones, digital cameras, MP3 players, laptops, GPS units, camcorders, and gaming consoles and the company will you pay you for them. Where possible Second Rotation refurbishes them and makes them available to its partners for resale. You can find used iPods on Target.com thanks to Second Rotation.

SOLES UNITED

Solesunited.com

Send in worn-out Croc shoes, and Soles United will recycle and refashion them into a new pair of Crocs that are donated to nonprofit organizations around the world. To date, Soles United has donated more than 1 million pairs of shoes made from recycled Crocs.

TERRACYCLE

Terracycle.net

Based in Trenton, New Jersey, TerraCycle is redefining America's relationship with its trash. The company that began with plant food made from worm poop and packaged in empty Pepsi bottles has exploded into an innovation powerhouse that transform garbage—like Oreo cookies and Chips Ahoy! wrappers—into a broad range of products, including office supplies, backpacks and messenger bags, and even shower curtains and umbrellas.

U.S. POSTAL SERVICE

Usps.com

In 2008, the U.S. Postal Service launched a pilot program at 1,500 post offices around the country to recycle consumers' small electronics and inkjet printer cartridges for free. At participating post offices, customers can use free envelopes to mail Blackberries, iPods, digital cameras, PDAs, and other electronic items without having to pay for postage.

Information/Education

THE LAZY ENVIRONMENTALIST

Lazyenvironmentalist.com/3rs

I've created a special page to keep Lazy Environmentalist readers updated about innovative ways to reduce, reuse and recycle. Find affordable, forward-thinking products and services that make it easier and easier to live by this mantra.

2

Style Made Simple

Wardrobe Revision

Eco-fashion is about more than your look;

it's about how your look came to be. Designers who choose to integrate planetary consciousness into their clothing collections ask important questions: What kind of fiber was used to make that T-shirt? What type of dye was used to color that skirt? How did those pants get to this store? But though more and more designers—both established and new—are designing clothing with an environmental eye, greening your closet on a budget is not as simple as taking a trip to the mall. Try tossing around green lingo like "ingeo," "soy," "bamboo," "cocona," or "organic cotton" in your local clothing store and check out the looks you get.

But it is possible to fill your closet with affordable, stylish clothing that was made responsibly. You simply have to know where to look. As with conventional fashion, environmentally minded clothing created by the world's top designers carries some of the world's top prices. So to keep his or her wardrobe up to date, the fashion-forward, budget-conscious Lazy Environmentalist must rely upon a knack for uncovering deals and a willingness to embrace new designers, business practices, and retailers. Here's some advice for choosing the right looks for you and the planet.

KNOW THE MATERIALS

Green fashion begins with eco-conscious fabrics, so it's important to know your materials. Currently there is a (growing) list of materials that are considered healthful and more sustainable for humans and the planet. Organic cotton is the most prevalent—and accessible—of the bunch, accounting for about 70 percent of all eco-fashion sales. Unlike its conventional counterpart, organic cotton is grown without the use of toxic pesticides and insecticides

—many of which are considered carcinogenic. Globally, 25 percent of all insecticides and 10 percent of all pesticides are sprayed on conventional cotton, so going organic not only removes the toxins from your T-shirts, underwear, and socks (and anything else made of cotton) but also eliminates a lot of poison from the environment. Fabrics made from other naturally grown crops like soy, corn (called "ingeo"), and bamboo are also considered earth-friendly because they grow and replenish rapidly. And many athletic garments include fabrics derived from coconut shells, which help moisture evaporate, absorb odor, enhance cooling, and provide UV protection. This wonder coconut fiber is called cocona, and it's currently being used by brands like Cannondale, Marmot, New Balance, and Champion.

On the other hand, synthetic fibers like nylon, spandex, and polyester are usually derived from oil, a finite resource that is presently at risk of being depleted and is also one of the main culprits of pollution and greenhouse gas emissions. But materials don't have to be grown to be earth friendly. Used plastic soda bottles made of PET (Polyethylene Terephthalate) can be recycled and transformed into polyester products such as strappy dresses, comfy T-shirts, or cozy fleece pullovers. Recycling materials for clothing (or anything else for that matter) is an environmental win because it reduces our dependence on virgin natural resources, reduces the amount of energy necessary to convert those natural resources into new products, and helps keep waste out of landfills. Less waste in landfills equals less methane released into the atmosphere (methane is a greenhouse gas that's 20 times more harmful than carbon dioxide and is produced as garbage decomposes). Designers and fashion labels that utilize greener fibers are quite literally a breath of fresh air.

EMBRACE NEW FASHION LABELS

Those of us determined to green our jeans will find that most eco-aware denim is priced at or above $150 a pair. But there are exceptions. Good Society delivers high-style, fair-trade certified organic cotton jeans for about $100. Not only is the styling clean and sharp, but every pair purchased also helps provide fair wages for the workers who produce them in India. When we think about "going green," we typically focus on reducing our environmental impact. But fair-trade certification also ensures that the people making the products we use are not exploited in the process. This helps to create a web of positive change—a good society, if you will. And for Aiden Dingh, Good Society's co-founder, it's not enough to sell clothing that respects both the people who make it and the environment we live in, it's also essential to make those items affordable. While Sling and Stones, Dingh's original organic cotton denim line, carries designer prices, Good Society makes eco-chic clothing accessible to a broader audience. You can find the collection at big national retailers like Urban Outfitters and at smaller boutiques across the country. Good Society keeps the good going by giving 10 percent of its profits to environmental causes.

As eco-aware designers are busy experimenting with new materials and inventive manufacturing techniques, some are also altering the traditional business model. Nvohk, a surf-inspired, eco-clothing company believes that business as usual is business as boring. Based on a model called "crowd-funding," nvohk customers—or "members," as the company calls them—contribute $50 and are able to vote on every major business decision like company logo design, clothing design, and even advertising. Once 60 percent of the members agree on a course of action, the management team implements the decision. Members receive a 25 percent discount on all products and collectively share in 35 percent of all net profits via reward points that can be redeemed for nvohk clothing (the company's corporate structure prohibits the distribution of cash to its members). The model is designed to accommodate 40,000 members, but the business plan went into effect in June 2008 when 3,000 members had registered via the company's website, Projectnvohk.com. Nvohk is market-based supply-and-demand economics set at mach speed: cutting out the middlemen and channeling customer preferences (demand) directly into manufacturing decisions (supply). Like any new concept, nvohk will undoubtedly attract a fair share of detractors, but several thousand people are already jumping at the chance to be part of a company that feeds the green economy by utilizing sustainable materials like organic cotton while donating 10 percent of net profits to environmental organizations.

CHECK THE ESTABLISHED FASHION LABELS

Inspired by the sophisticated creations of the eco-fashion community, familiar fashion labels are also beginning to strut their eco-stuff. Guess and Eileen Fisher are among the brands debuting stylish, organic cotton collections. While not necessarily the most affordable way to green your wardrobe, these fashion labels get points for making green choices accessible to everyday shoppers. And bargain hunters know that big label items often end up on the racks at TJ Maxx and Marshall's, so that ultimate green deal may already be waiting for you.

You don't have to look hard to find a deal at Levi's. The most trusted name in denim reminds us that boutique brands aren't the only way to give your jeans an eco-boost. The Levis Eco collection features boot cut, straight, and slim cuts for men and women with prices that hover around $68 per pair (though if you head over to J.C. Penney you can usually find them on sale for closer to $40. J.C. Penney also offers Arizona Jeans's new eco-collection at irresistible prices. Instead of tossing the cotton in a landfill that's left over from its cotton mill, Arizona Jeans recycles it into jeans that retail for around $40 per pair. The company does the same thing with T-shirts. Incorporating 60 percent recycled cotton, the Ts can be yours for $20 each.

The ultimate in organic cotton basics can be found at Los Angeles–based American Apparel. The clothing manufacturer pays its workforce fair, living wages to produce a sexy, youthful organic line that has moved away from earthy beige and is now available in a rainbow of colors. American Apparel's snug-fit organic cotton Ts retail for $18 and are available in black, white, pomegranate pink, galaxy blue, dijon yellow, or cinder grey. The bright colors are also available in long-sleeve Ts, underwear, and one-pieces for babies and dogs. Visit Americanapparel.net to view the entire "Sustainable Edition" collection.

Summer Rayne Oakes is a model-activist, sustainability strategist, and author of *Style Naturally: The Savvy Shopping Guide to Sustainable Fashion and Beauty*. She has also teamed up with Payless to launch the company's eco-friendly Zoe & Zac collection.

How did you first hit upon the idea of using fashion as a medium for creating positive environmental change?
I was looking for an outlet back in 2001 to connect my environmental studies to people who normally didn't have these issues on their radar screens. Most of my buddies in college weren't the enviro types, so I needed cool outlets to get people to understand and care. Fashion is incredibly linguistic; it's very media-friendly, so it was a perfect outlet to communicate hard-to-understand issues in sustainability. I found out that it could be an incredible tool not just to communicate the issues but also to foster real change for millions of people—whether that meant going organic, buying fair trade, or reducing carbon miles from manufacturing to point of sale.

Why is it so important to help companies like Payless go green?
It's awesome to work with Payless on their sustainability initiatives and their green shoe line, Zoe & Zac. The whole idea behind it is to "democratize" green which means scaling it up and making it afford-able to more people. Often green products and services are only avail-able to an elite few, so it's important to build the infrastructure that makes it possible for everyone to participate. What's also great is that while this green initiative is epitomized outwardly in a shoe, we're also beginning to create internal metrics and use sustainability as a source of innovation across Collective Brand's (Payless' parent com-pany) other product lines. Sustainable change doesn't happen over-night. It's an evolution.

As an environmental activist do you feel it's appropriate to strive to be "Dressed to Kill?"
As much as I love schlepping around in sweats and a tee, keeping up

appearances is important in making a good impression even for the baddest-ass environmentalists. I almost exclusively wear pieces that are refurbished or are more ecologically or socially conscious. I seek out items with a purpose. And the cool thing is that the sustainable fashion industry has matured so much and has become more affordable, so it's available to anyone who wants to live it, wear it, be it.

To stock up on trendy organic cotton duds at rock-bottom prices, hit your local H&M. The company continually features eco-clothing for the entire family. The products may be super affordable, but that doesn't mean that H&M mistreats the employees at its many factories around the globe. Quite the opposite in fact—as a member of the Fair Labor Association, H&M routinely receives high marks for its socially responsible practices. On the environmental front, the retailer has steadily increased its use of organic cotton from 40 tons in 2005 to 1,700 tons in its spring 2008 collection. That number is set to increase by 50% in 2009 as H&M also begins introducing clothing for men and women made from recycled cotton, wool, and polyester.

ENTER THE BIG BOX RETAILERS
There is no company on Earth that can match the purchasing power of Wal-Mart, the largest retailer in the world. So when the company decided that the environment was an important issue and that consumers should have easy access to affordable eco-minded products, big changes happened. Today Wal-Mart is the world's largest purchaser of organic cotton, which it spins into 100 percent organic cotton pajamas for adults and complete organic cotton lines for children. Wal-Mart also features Coca-Cola's Drink2Wear line of T-shirts made from 50 percent recycled Coca-Cola bottles, retailing for under $8 apiece and featuring witty eco-slogans like "Rehash Your Trash."

Target is also going green. In 2008, the company teamed up with eco-fashion designer Rogan Gregory to offer a limited-edition organic designer collection. Gregory is known for Loomstate, his organic denim line, as well as for his collaboration with Bono and his wife, Ali Hewson, on the socially responsible fashion label Edun. Through Target, Rogan introduced a 100-piece eco-fashion collection at prices most shoppers could afford. Within days of hitting store shelves, the collection was sold out, sending a resounding message to the fashion industry that consumers will shop green when the products are good and the price is right. Hopefully more companies will follow Target's lead.

EMBRACE REUSE

As discussed in Chapter 1 (The 3Rs: Reduce, Reuse & Recycle), fashionistas who are bored with their wardrobes can refresh their look without consuming new products. This money-saving strategy also helps to reduce the amount of materials that go into new products as well the energy required to make and ship them. Tattered jeans can be successfully repaired—not just patched—by Denim Therapy at its facility in Cincinnati. For $7 per inch of repair plus $12 for shipping, experts will repair holes and rips and restore the look and feel of your jeans by considering the unique thread weight, fade, wash, pattern, weave, wear, and look of your go-to pair. Pop your jeans in the mail, and they'll be back to you and better than ever in just two to three weeks.

Wardrobe fatigue is the primary reason we ditch our old clothes and rush out to buy new duds. But what if we connected with others who are also uninspired by the contents of their closets? Sure, you can host a clothing swap in your living room, but the invitees will be limited to those you know—how predictable! Swapstyle.com allows you to expand your swapping potential by connecting with a vast database of those with garb to barter. The best part? Swapstyle.com transactions are money-free—all you ever pay is postage. After you've created an account, you simply start listing the products you have available to trade. Members who dig your duds will contact you to see if you'd like to swap for something they have (you, of course, can do the same). Once a match is made, ship off your goods and welcome your new pair of

True Religion jeans or Stella McCartney shoes and whatever else completes your look.

Vintage clothing shops are also Reuse emporiums—the preferred destinations for snagging choice clothing and accessories at affordable prices. These days vintage shops are stocking much more than bowling shirts and pristine purple jumpsuits. You'll find items that spice up your everyday wardrobe and maybe even a piece or two that can be worn to the office. Don't have time to comb the racks at each location? The folks at Sprig.com and Jargol.com have done the work for you. Check out their lists of the best vintage shops in the United States and worldwide.

HUNT DOWN DEALS

Before you set out to score a new eco-look, check to see whether online deals and discounts are available. WhiteApricot.com is an excellent resource for locating bargains. The website's editors handpick deals on eco-clothing, shoes, and accessories, as well as organic skin care, natural cosmetics, and other stylish green products that are up to 50 percent less than retail prices. Savings can be instantaneously yours on clothing and accessories from illustrious eco-fashion labels like Stewart & Brown, Deborah Lindquist, Terra Planna, and Ecoist. Some offers are exclusive and can only be found on WhiteApricot.com or through the company's email newsletter (sign up for it today to get first dibs on new discounts).

No time to hunt for deals? You can always borrow your way to a killer eco-outfit. The right accessory may be just what you need. Bag Borrow or Steal (bagborroworsteal.com) lends users designer handbags, purses, jewelry, sunglasses, and other accessories at a fraction of the price of what it would cost to own. If you absolutely must have Chanel's 2.55 quilted bag, but are made dizzy by the $2,500+ price tag, borrow it for a week for $160 and give it back when you're done. Impress your date, dazzle the parents, or wow your boss while respecting your wallet and protecting the planet (borrowing gives others the chance to use the same item, which reduces our overall eco-impact).

Fashion Labels

AMERICAN APPAREL

Americanapparel.net

For the ultimate in organic cotton basics, turn to American Apparel. The clothing manufacturer pays its workforce fair, living wages to produce a sexy, youthful organic line that has moved away from earthy beige and is now available in a rainbow of colors.

ARIZONA JEANS

Azjeans.com

Arizona Jeans's new eco-collection is available at J.C. Penney. Instead of tossing in a landfill the cotton that's left over from the cotton mill, Arizona Jeans recycles it into jeans that retail for around $40 per pair. The company does the same thing with T-shirts, incorporating 60 percent recycled cotton. They can be yours for $20.

BAGIR

Bagir.com

This menswear company has leapfrogged to the forefront of affordable and sustainable style with its collection of eco-suits, which were introduced at Sears in 2008. The EcoGir collection features suits made of partially and 100 percent recycled materials that can also be machine-washed to avoid the need for dry cleaning.

BILLABONG

billabong.com

Whether you're looking for polo shirts made of organic cotton and stylized with bold graphics or funky board shorts made from recycled soda bottles, Billabong keeps the outdoor-oriented set moving in eco-style. Visit the website to find a list of participating retailers. Dogfunk.com is one such retailer that carries Billabong's eco-offerings at budget-friendly prices.

EILEEN FISHER

Eileenfisher.com

Eileen Fisher has boldly ventured into the world of organic cotton. Available at major retailers ranging from Nordstrom to TJ Maxx, Eileen Fisher offers plenty of age-appropriate shapes and styles. Eco-fashion newcomers can ease into the green fashion movement through items from this dependable and trusted brand.

GINA MICHELE
Ginamichele.com
Fun, feminine, and effortlessly chic, Gina Michele's Verde collection of dresses are made of soft bamboo jersey. Michele is being increasingly recognized for her ability to merge art with function. Now add eco-responsibility to the mix too. Prices start at just under $100.

GOOD SOCIETY
Goodsociety.org
Good Society delivers high-style, fair-trade certified organic cotton jeans for men and women, with prices ranging around $100. The styling is clean and sharp, and every pair purchased helps provide fair wages for the workers who produce them in India. Find them at Urban Outfitters and eco-boutiques around the country.

H&M
Hm.com
Stock up on affordable and trendy organic cotton duds for the entire family at your local H&M, a company that has steadily increased its use of organic cotton from 40 tons in 2005 to 1,700 tons in its spring 2008 collection. That number is set to increase by 50% in 2009 as H&M also begins introducing clothing for men and women made from recycled cotton, wool, and polyester.

LEVIS
Levis.com
Levis keeps it green with its 100 percent organic cotton Levis Eco denim collection featuring boot cut, straight, and slim cuts for men and women with prices that hover around $68 per pair.

MELISSA
Melissaaustralia.com.au
Melissa was started in Brazil 25 years ago and has since sold 50 million shoes made entirely of Melflex, a pliable, hypoallergenic, and odor-free recycled plastic material. The company's eco-mission extends beyond its footwear—99.9 percent of used water and waste generated at its factory gets recycled.

NVOHK
Nvohk.com
Based on a business model called crowd-funding, nvohk is a surf-inspired, eco-clothing company that's directed by the thousands of members who collectively own it. Members receive a 25 percent discount on all apparel, which

is made from organic cotton and other sustainable fabrics, and collectively share in 35 percent of all net profits via reward points that can be redeemed for nvohk products.

Reuse Resources

BAG BORROW OR STEAL
Bagborroworsteal.com
Bag Borrow or Steal lends users designer handbags, purses, jewelry, sunglasses, and other accessories at a fraction of the price of what it would cost to own. In the movie *Sex and the City,* Carrie asks her new assistant, Louise, how she can afford such a fabulous new Louis Vuitton, to which Louise replies, "Bagborroworsteal.com."

DENIM THERAPY
Denimtherapy.com
Tattered jeans can be successfully repaired and restored by Denim Therapy at its facility in Cincinnati. For about $7 per inch of repair (plus $12 shipping), denim therapists will repair holes and rips and restore the look and feel of your jeans by considering the unique thread weight, fade, wash, pattern, weave, wear, and look of your go-to pair. Pop your jeans in the mail, and they'll be back to you and better than ever in just two to three weeks.

EVINTAGE SOCIETY
Evintagesociety.com
Start your exploration into the realm of vintage clothing at eVintage Society, an online vintage sellers' collective featuring more than 45 vintage retailers. You can shop at their stores and peruse their blogs to learn more about their passion for recycling, preservation, and reinvention of vintage clothing to accommodate all types of fashion sensibilities.

SWAP STYLE
Swapstyle.com
Swapstyle.com is like browsing through thousands of people's closets and picking out only the things you absolutely have to have. Swap accessories, cosmetics, and shoes with fashionistas all over the globe for free. All you pay is the price of shipping.

QUIKSILVER

Quiksilver.com

Guys and girls will dig the vibrant, fresh designs that are increasingly made of organic cotton by Quiksilver. From stylish tees to denim jeans, Quiksilver is rapidly introducing eco-friendly products that are sure to be a hit in dorms rooms everywhere.

ZOE & ZAC

Payless.com

Get ready for some fantastic deals for under $30 on fashionable footwear and accessories made from materials like organic cotton, hemp, and linen. Zoe & Zac is a new line from Payless available at 500 stores nationwide as well as online through the company's website. Eco-fashion model and green guru Summer Rayne Oakes is the eco-consultant on the project, so you know it's going to look good.

Ones to Watch

PATAGONIA

Patagonia.com

Patagonia has long been an eco-leader in the clothing industry. For years, the company has used 100 percent organic cotton in its casual and performance lines for men, women, and kids. It also uses lots of recycled materials, namely PET, a polyester fabric made from recycled soda bottles. In 2005, Patagonia started its Common Threads Garment Recycling Program, which enables the company to recycle its customers' used Patagonia garments into new Patagonia garments and thus greatly reduce the need for virgin materials. Buy it, wear it, and give it back to the company when you're done with it so it can be made into something new. That's a truly enlightened eco-business model.

ROGAN GREGORY FOR TARGET

Target.com

In 2008, Target teamed up with fashion designer Rogan Gregory to offer a limited-edition organic designer collection. Gregory is known for Loomstate, his organic denim line, as well as for his collaboration with Bono and his wife, Ali Hewson, on the socially responsible fashion label Edun. Within days of hitting store shelves, Rogan's 100-piece eco-collection was sold out, sending a resounding message to the fashion industry that consumers will shop green when the products are good and the price is right.

SUMMER RAYNE OAKES

Summerrayneoakes.com

Model, author, social entrepreneur, television host, and all around environmental rock star Summer Rayne Oakes leverages her beauty and brains to catalyze social and environmental change throughout the fashion industry. Her book, *Style Naturally: The Savvy Shopping Guide to Sustainable Fashion and Beauty*, is a must-read for both fashion insiders and eco-minded consumers. Oakes has also joined forces with Payless to bring affordable eco-friendly footwear and accessories to the masses through the company's Zoe & Zac collection.

WAL-MART

Walmart.com/earth

Wal-Mart is the world's largest purchaser of organic cotton, which it spins into 100 percent organic cotton pajamas for adults and complete organic cotton lines for children. Wal-Mart also features Coca-Cola's Drink2Wear line of T-shirts, made from 50 percent recycled Coca-Cola bottles, retailing for under $8 apiece and featuring witty eco-slogans like "Rehash Your Trash."

Information/Education

CHARTREUSE CHIC

Chartreusechic.blogspot.com

Eco-friendly fashionistas will relish the insights, reporting, and sweet eco-finds touted throughout this blog, which is dedicated to covering the green fashion world. A quick search function lets you read up on your favorite eco-designers. Links to many of the best eco-boutiques are also readily accessible.

FABULOUSLY GREEN

Fabgreen.com

If it's the latest in green fashion and design you're searching for, then Fabulously Green will rank high on your list. Daily updates are complemented by features like a quick drop-down menu that lets you zero in on the latest news about your favorite eco-designers.

G SPOTTING

Gspotting.net

Founded by Lazy Environmentalist team member Margaret Teich, G Spotting covers the unexpected side of green innovation in pop culture, funky fashion, nail polish, and hip hop. Discover how Teich and her Generation Y peers are pushing green into the mainstream.

THE LAZY ENVIRONMENTALIST

Lazyenvironmentalist.com / style

I've created a special page to keep Lazy Environmentalist readers updated about ongoing trends in the world of eco-fashion. Discover the most afford-able and convenient ways to choose the right looks for you and the planet.

SPRIG

Sprig.com

Find lots of great content and commentary on green fashion, beauty, food, and home furnishings at this well-designed site that's owned by *Washington Post/Newsweek*. Editor Jeanie Pyun and her team keep the green insights coming on a daily basis. Check out the "Meet an Expert" section for inter-views with today's top green innovators.

STYLE WILL SAVE US

Stylewillsaveus.com

The UK-based digital magazine "for a peachy life" focuses on uber-stylish, organic, ethical, fair-trade, eco-friendly, vintage, recycled, and sustainable fashion. Follow the trends, read interviews with industry insiders, and learn how style will save you, me, and everybody.

THREAD

Bbc.co.uk / thread

Leave it to the UK's BBC to introduce the most fun online eco-fashion maga-zine. Click on the moving pictures to read about hot eco-designers and cool sustainable trends. View photo slide-shows and videos, and get tips on devel-oping your own personal eco-style.

WHITE APRICOT

Whiteapricot.com

Discover bargains and deals on eco-clothing, shoes, and accessories, as well as organic skin care, natural cosmetics, and other stylish green products that save up to 50 percent off retail prices. Some offers are exclusive and can only be found on WhiteApricot.com or through the company's email newsletter.

3

Tread Lightly **Another Take** on Transportation

When it comes to picking a vehicle, the smart choice for the planet is very often the smart choice for your wallet. That's because the more expensive your new car, the worse it typically performs on gas mileage. This means you pay more at the pump, and your car emits more greenhouse gas emissions into the atmosphere. Conversely, the most affordable cars on the road almost always cost the least to operate, get the best fuel economy, and release the fewest greenhouse gases. Of course, notable exceptions do apply. There's always the 100 percent gas-free electric-powered Tesla Roadster—the ride of choice for folks like the Google founders and George Clooney.

We may not run multibillion-dollar companies or own a villa on Lake Como, but we still have access to plenty of cars that run efficiently while respecting the environment and our budget. But what makes a car an affordable eco-choice? The definition of "affordable" is of course subjective, but the average U.S. consumer currently pays more than $28,000 for a new car (according to numbers released by research firm Comerica Incorporated). So, while not a perfect science, we'll consider cars priced below $28,000 to be accessible for the average consumer. And by my calculations, a car that averages more than 30 miles per gallon (mpg) demonstrates particularly strong eco-credibility. Factor in the two criteria—cost plus miles per gallon—adjust for style and versatility, and there are quite a few cars that still make the cut.

GREEN YOUR RIDE: GAS-POWERED CARS

Hip, green automobile affordability starts with the nimble lineup of sub-$15,000 hatchbacks gaining popularity across the United States. While many vehicles in this class fall just below our 30 mpg threshold—based on the adjusted mpg standards introduced by the Environmental Protection Agency in 2008—the Honda Fit, a new generation of mega-versatile hatchback (starting msrp [Manufacturers Suggested Retail Price]: $13,950; combined mpg 31), not only surpasses the mark, but does so with style and smarts. Honda placed the gas tank under the front passenger seat, which allows the back seats to fold flush to the floor. This gives the streamlined caravan a surprisingly roomy cargo space and opens it up to multiple passenger/storage configurations. Kids, camping gear, groceries, pets—they'll all fit in the Fit (sorry, couldn't resist). Honda has entered the next level of affordable design with a car that's earth-, family-, and iPod-friendly—just plug it right into the stereo system. But don't take it from me. *Motor Trend Magazine* calls the Fit "the right choice for the enthusiast who wants a car that handles twisties as well as it does chores, saves gas, and eases your budget."

A newcomer to the hatchback scene is a car so unique it almost defies categorization. Building upon the success of the MINI Cooper (starting msrp: $18,050; combined mpg: 32) MINI has introduced the MINI Clubman (starting msrp: $19,950; combined mpg: 32), an equally fun ride in a body that accommodates more passengers and more stuff. The Clubman is fast. The Clubman is cool. The Clubman also has a unique club door. In addition to two regular front doors, the car has one narrow door on the right side that's used as a backseat entrance. The Clubman's trunk is also original, with two barn doors that open outward to the sides.

These righteous hatchbacks achieve top-flight fuel economy in two ways. First, they trade excessive power for supreme efficiency (while they've got above average pick-up, they're probably not the best for street-legal drag racing—unless souped-up, of course). Second, these cars are lightweight. They're still safe, but weigh about 2,000 pounds less than beefier sedans and station wagons. Remember what it felt like when the hefty class bully jumped on your back for a piggyback ride? That's how a car engine feels when lurching forward under the weight of the typical luxury sedan or station wagon. Car engines propelling heavier loads expend more energy, consume more fuel, and release more greenhouse gases than when tucked inside nimble, lightweight, lower-priced vehicles.

To see another example of this logic, check out the Smart Car. The mini vehicles arrived in the States in 2008 to offer commuters yet another fun, affordable, fuel-efficient option. The Smart Fortwo (starting msrp: $11,590; combined mpg: 36) comes in both hard-top and convertible models, both of which deliver unprecedented levels of joy each time you slide the minute vehicle into the narrowest of parking spots. Originally developed in Europe as a joint venture between Swatch (yup, the watch company) and Mercedes-Benz, the Smart Fortwo's colorful, attractive design reflects its heritage. And thanks to German engineering, the Fortwo's small engine can rev up to 90 miles per hour, so even if highway driving is part of your daily commute, this little car will get you where you want to go.

For a little more car, top-flight fuel efficiency, and prices that won't break the bank, consider today's more affordable hybrid car models—automobiles that run on a combination of gasoline and electric-powered engines. The Toyota Prius (starting msrp: $21,500; combined mpg: 46), Toyota Camry Hybrid (starting msrp: $25,350; combined mpg: 34), Honda Civic Hybrid (starting msrp: $22,600; combined mpg: 42), and Nissan Altima Hybrid (starting msrp: $25,170; combined mpg: 34) are some of the top picks. If you prefer your green transportation conspicuous, go with the Prius. Everyone on the road will acknowledge you as a super-conscious, enlightened hero of the planet. If you prefer a less obvious eco-ride, then opt for the Camry, Civic, or Altima hybrids. No one will notice your laudable environmental efforts. They'll just assume that you dig smart, sensible cars. And be on the lookout for new, affordably priced hybrid models from Honda like the 2009 Honda Insight which is slated to become the lowest priced hybrid available. The Japanese car maker no longer finds it acceptable that its compatriot Toyota controls nearly 70 percent of the U.S. hybrid market. Their rivalry for hybrid supremacy bodes extremely well for cost-conscious consumers and for the planet.

Diesel-powered cars are also making an eco-comeback, thanks to German engineering. Developed in partnership among Mercedes, Audi, and Volkswagen, a new diesel technology called BLUETEC enables car manufacturers to build diesel-powered cars clean enough to pass the stringent vehicle emissions standards of all 50 U.S. states. Diesel-powered cars get significantly better gas mileage—about 20 to 40 percent better—than their standard gasoline-powered counterparts. Lazy Environmentalists can check out the 2009 Volkswagen Jetta TDI, available as both a sedan (starting msrp: $22,640; combined mpg: 34) and SportWagen (starting msrp: $23,590; combined mpg: 34). Both combine turbocharged high-performance with crisp power-assisted rack-and-pinion steering. Strap your little ones in the backseat of the SportWagen, throw all the gear in the roomy trunk, and head out for some quality family time. The SportWagen is the eco-friendly antidote for young parents who mistakenly believe that traveling in an SUV is the only way to keep children safe while stowing all their gear.

Fuel-efficient gasoline, diesel, and hybrid engines help reduce our environmental impact, but they still keep us dependent on fossil fuels. That's why concerted efforts have been undertaken over the last few years to introduce biofuels—fuels made from biomass like corn, soybeans, and sugarcane instead of petroleum—like biodiesel and ethanol. As research into the environmental merits of these fuels continues, biodiesel is looking like an eco-winner. It can significantly reduce air pollutants and greenhouse gas emissions by about 76 percent over regular diesel fuel (factoring its entire lifecycle from farm field to gas tank). The results for ethanol, a potential alternative to regular gasoline, are less clear. Derived primarily from corn in the United States (though predominantly and successfully from sugarcane in Brazil), ethanol production is purported to require more energy to produce than it actually provides. While it may burn cleaner than regular gasoline and generate fewer greenhouse gas emissions, making it from corn appears to be a losing proposition. Both biodiesel and ethanol production may also contribute to higher global food prices as land that once grew food is converted to grow fuel crops. Reports are also emerging about tropical forests that are being destroyed to make way for soybean or palm oil plantations to produce biofuels. While perhaps done with good intentions, this is ecologically counterintuitive, as tropical forests support biodiversity, release essential oxygen into the atmosphere, and help the planet manage carbon dioxide emissions by storing it in their root systems.

In response to these concerns, energy companies are aggressively researching alternative ways to create biofuels. Researchers are developing methods of manufacturing biodiesel in laboratories from nonfood sources like algae. Others are collecting waste veggie oil from restaurants and repurposing it for use as biodiesel in our cars. On the ethanol front, companies are exploring the potential of cellulosic ethanol fuel—created from nonfood plant sources like switchgrass and even waste products like wood chips. No one knows exactly when these types of solutions will be readily available on a large, convenient, and accessible scale, but some of the smartest minds in this country and around the world are working overtime to see that these solutions arrive sooner than later.

CHOOSE TWO WHEELS: MOTOR SCOOTERS

Yet another way to avoid pain at the pump, keep your greenhouse gas emissions in check, and still enjoy the freedom of the road is on a rugged, stylish motor scooter. Two-wheeled motor scooters can accelerate quickly, navigate traffic easily, and squeeze into parking spaces that turn automobiles green with envy. They also save a bundle on gasoline—motor scooters typically average between 60 and 80 mpg. While Vespa scooters are most famous for their exceptional quality and iconic Italian design, other nimble, well-designed, and more affordable scooters can also rescue you from the expense of your daily commute.

Aprilia's line of Scarabeo motor scooters traces its heritage back to the post-WWII era and to the town of Noale in the Italian province of Venice. Renowned for its success on motorcycle racing circuits around the globe, Aprilia brings the same attention to detail and unique styling to the Scarabeo line. The Scarabeo 200 is a superbly crafted urban commuter that tops out near 80 mph and

Neil Saiki is founder and CTO of Zero Motorcycles, a company that makes high-performance electric motorcycles.

How did you get the idea for Zero Motorcycles?
I worked on a team that designed a turbo prop "spy plane," one of which was sold to National Geographic to do ozone layer research. That was my awakening to global environmental issues. I also did a transportation study while working for NASA in the early 1990s, when it became clear to me that electric vehicles were the right solution. A few years later, while working on mountain bike designs for companies like Santa Cruz, Mountain Cycle, and Haro, I began looking into making an electric motorcycle, but it was clear that the heavy, low-capacity batteries in use at the time were not appropriate. So when the new generation of lithium-ion batteries started to become available, I began working on what would eventually become the Zero X motorcycle.

What is Zero Motorcycles's positive environmental impact?
The Zero X has just 1/8th the carbon footprint per mile of a regular gasoline-powered motorcycle and generates just 1/100th of the smog-producing nitrous oxides. It also reduces noise pollution because it is very quiet while riding.

Which is fastest—a Zero X, a Zero S, or a cheetah?
The cheetah, but just barely.

a delivers a whopping 70 mpg. Its large 16-inch wheels provide stability and a sense of overall safety and at $3,399 it truly combines performance and affordability.

For a high-quality ride with retro flair and an even more affordable price point, check out the Yamaha Vino. The Vino 125 sells for $2,899 and averages 96 miles per gallon. The four-stroke engine delivers plenty of pep and a top speed of around 55 miles per hour. Or quench your thirst for the open road and the feel of wind (or maybe a light breeze) pressing against your face with the Vino Classic, an entry-level 49cc scooter that sells for $2,049 and delivers 112 miles per gallon. Its maximum speed of 35 miles per hour will, in many cases, get you comfortably to work, class, or the grocery store. The Honda Metropolitan delivers similar performance in a more compact frame and retails for $2,049. Other affordable motor scooter models worth looking into are available from Piaggio and Kymco.

PLUG IT IN: ELECTRIC VEHICLES

In response to global warming and soaring fuel costs, young, upstart companies around the globe are working overtime to bring affordable electric cars to market and almost entirely remove gasoline from the automotive equation. One such example is TH!NK Global, a company originally owned by Ford but now the brainchild of a Norwegian iconoclastic genius named Jan-Olaf Willums. TH!NK plans to deliver its peppy compact electric car to the U.S. market by the end of 2009. With a top speed of 65 miles per hour and a 110-mile range per charge, the TH!NK *city* considers your wallet (you can own one starting at around $25,000) and your style (the streamlined design features side indicator lights, strong wheel arches, and a variety of striking colors), without forsaking the environment.

Here's how: Cars fueled by gasoline create about 20 pounds of carbon dioxide greenhouse gas emissions with every gallon used. And while electric-powered cars, which run on electricity stored in their rechargeable batteries, are not a total environmental win—plugging them into a wall socket uses power generated from environmentally damaging fossil fuels like coal—they are still the cleaner alternative. That's because coal burned in a power plant is much more efficient at generating energy than the gasoline that powers your car. Studies by the California Air Resources Board have also shown that when charging on the regular power grid, electric cars are a significantly healthier planetary alternative to gasoline-powered cars. Proponents of electric cars also argue that gas-free vehicles present an exciting opportunity to run our cars using clean, renewable energy sources like wind and solar. This means that if solar panels powered your home, solar energy could be charging your electric car every time you plug it in. It's a great plan—one that we'll be sure to implement as solar energy and other clean energy sources become more affordable (see Chapter 4: Energy).

When it comes to electric, four wheels aren't the only way to drive. The Aptera Typ-1 electric-powered three-wheeler will redefine your expectations of what an automobile can look like. With an egg-shaped body, funky dashboard, built-in rooftop solar panels, and front wheel spokes that protrude from the body (for stability), the Typ-1 conjures images of lunar explorations. But this is no moon mobile. This is an everyday vehicle that will comfortably take two adults where they need to go (there's a smaller seat in the back for a petite third passenger). The Typ-1 scores extra points with doors that open upward, Lamborghini style, and an ability to reach speeds of up to 90 miles per hour. The all-electric version gets 120 miles per charge. A plug-in hybrid electric model (PHEV) ramps that closer to a mind-bending 300 miles per gallon (see discussion of PHEVs below). Is it affordable? Starting at around $27,000, that's a judgment call you'll have to make.

Three may be the new four when it comes to electric, but two is always cool. With models like the Zero X from Zero Motorcycles, which goes from zero to 30 mph in just two seconds, electric motorcycles are another enticing eco-option. Top speed on this off-road motorcycle is just under 60 miles per hour. The electric battery pack delivers about 40 miles per charge, and the lightweight, zero-emission frame ensures that those miles are going to be ridiculously fun. The Zero X is also nearly silent, which has professional motorcross speedways and racing promoters—subject to strict noise ordinances—working to get these motorcycles on their tracks. As for cost, the Zero X will set you back just $7,450 for the standard model (competitive with conventional 250cc gasoline-powered motorcycles in its class) and long-term savings are guaranteed, since plugging into the power grid only takes two hours and costs about a penny per mile. Plus, you never have to pay for oil changes because, well, there is no oil. Zero Motorcycles is also preparing to release the Zero S, a street legal electric motorcycle that lets you channel your inner Evel Knievel into your daily commute.

No conversation about electric vehicles would be complete without a word on plug-in hybrid electric vehicles (PHEVs). Touted as one of the best solutions for combating global warming, PHEVs can help us embrace the future without having to completely relinquish the past. PHEVs look like normal cars, but can be plugged into any regular outlet to recharge their onboard battery, which, depending upon the size, can get up to 60 miles per charge. While the cars can still be fueled by gasoline for extended trips, most day-to-day commuting and errands can be handled by the electric motor. Prominent advocates include James Hansen, a NASA climate scientist; Chris Paine, director of *Who Killed The Electric Car?*; and Al Gore, the guy who inspired the world to care about the planet instead of becoming president. PHEVs aren't on the road just yet, but look for the Saturn VUE SUV plug-in electric hybrid in late 2009. Ford and Toyota are also developing PHEV models, and General Motors should have its highly anticipated Chevy Volt PHEV on the streets by 2010.

OTHER WAYS TO RIDE

Fuel-efficient cars are great for combating global warming. Electric-powered vehicles are even better. But nothing beats taking the bus. When it comes to going green on a budget, opting for public transportation is the surest way to reduce your eco-impact. This isn't a news flash. As the environmental community has reminded us for years, public transportation—combined with walking and/or biking—is a surefire path to eco-enlightenment. It's been proven. A study from the Environmental Law & Policy Center (ELPC) found that a bus carrying just seven passengers is more fuel-efficient (read: eco-friendly) than the average car. A full bus is six times more efficient. And a full train is 15 times more fuel-efficient than the average vehicle.

But millions of us have yet to ditch our cars for the bus or the subway or the train. Life without a vehicle saves us money by liberating us from car payments, insurance premiums, sky-high gas prices, and general maintenance bills. That's obvious. But it's not enough. There has to be something else—a perk of sorts—that would make public transportation (or walking or biking) so enticing that we would have no choice but to leave our cars behind.

Free Internet access would be a start. Logging on while commuting would alter the nature of the nine-to-five hustle. Instead of spending their morning journey wishing they were still in bed, commuters would be able to finish that report before the early meeting, catch up on email, join an online game of Texas Hold 'Em, or whatever it is that one does with the World Wide Web. And in more than 20 cities across America, Wi-Fi-equipped public transportation is no longer a fantasy. Bus fare in places like Cincinnati, Reno, Austin, Albuquerque, Colorado Springs, San Francisco, and Seattle increasingly grants riders unlimited access to the Internet.

Wi-Fi is spreading to trains too. In Massachusetts, the 45-mile rail line connecting Worchester and Boston recently added free public Wi-Fi. And commuters are digging it. Kriss Erickson, deputy chief of staff for the Massachusetts Bay Transportation Authority, says that adding wireless Internet access is "probably the most well-received enhancement that we've ever done." Plans are now under way to add Wi-Fi to all of Boston's commuter rail lines. Santa Fe and Salt Lake City are not far behind.

Public transportation is best, but cars can still fit into a Lazy Environmentalist lifestyle if you drive them the right way—that is, full to capacity. The more passengers in the car, the lower the individual eco-impact of each person. That's because sharing rides helps take cars off the road, and fewer cars on the road means fewer greenhouse gas emissions (can I get an "Amen!"). A good place to find additional passengers who are going your way is Zimride.com, a company founded on the simple idea that strangers are more likely to share rides with each other if they can be made to feel comfortable before they meet. To meet those needs, Zimride has created a social networking platform that enables members to create personal profiles and select ride mates who share similar music tastes, favorite sports teams, or who just seem "normal." Zimmers can also evaluate things like driving speed, music volume, and smoking preferences before agreeing to hop in. In addition to finding rides at Zimride.com, the Zimride Facebook application makes the ride-sharing service readily available to Facebook's 80 million users.

It works well. People save money by sharing on gas and tolls (or avoiding the costs of buses, trains, and planes), reach their desired destinations without driving their own cars, and make plenty of new friends along the way, as testimonials on the website can attest. Zimride is also a great tool for companies looking to organize employee carpooling, local sports teams that want to drive to practice together, and any other group that needs a centralized site to coordinate ride sharing.

Zimride is one of many vehicle-oriented services that consider the environment and your budget. RideAmigos.com is for those who want to share taxicabs anywhere around the world. PickUpPal.com combines ride sharing with package delivery—earn a little extra cash while you consolidate trips. And Shareling.com connects travelers looking to share a road trip—the website's interactive maps show available rides across the globe. What better way to get from Cairo to Karachi on a Lazy Environmentalist budget? While Zimride makes ride sharing easy and stress-free, NuRide ups the ante by offering you rewards for sharing rides. The service operates just like an airline membership rewards program. The more rides you share, the more points you earn and the more value you can redeem. Partners include Applebee's, Austin Grill, and Ringling Brothers and Barnum & Bailey Circus. If that's not motivation to find some passengers, I don't know what is.

John Zimmer is co-founder and COO of Zimride, a company that makes ride sharing easy, fun, cost-saving, and reliable.

How did you get the idea for Zimride?
Sitting in my college dorm on the East Coast while Logan Green was doing the same on the West Coast, we were both astonished by the incredibly inefficient automobile transportation system in the country based on one car carrying only one person on its journey. We felt we had the tools in front of us to do something about it. Zimride taps the potential of social networks such as Facebook to unlock one of the major barriers to the mainstream adoption of carpooling—developing higher levels of trust between people. Two individuals who share a common network, friend, interest, or affiliation will feel much more comfortable with each other and are much more likely to share a ride.

What is Zimride's positive environmental impact?
Reducing the number of cars on the road by getting two or more people in a car versus single occupancy has tremendous power to reduce overall automobile emissions. Through Zimride, members have already collectively reduced carbon dioxide emissions by more than one million pounds, and as more people use the service more often, this positive trend accelerates. Additionally, Zimriding demonstrates that being "green" can be fun, convenient, and social and can save individuals a great deal of money.

I hear you're fond of dressing up like a chicken? What's the deal?!
It actually was as a "Happy Beaver." We figured that beavers all over the world would be a lot happier if people started to Zimride. So, I dressed up as a Happy Beaver and my friend dressed up as Frog Prince, and we ran around Cornell University's campus telling people about Zimride. It worked! More than 3,500 students and staff are Zimriding at Cornell, saving the community more than $200,000, reducing carbon dioxide emission by more than 300,000 pounds, and making many beavers happy.

Then there's the vanpool. That's right. The vanpool. The rising popularity of ride sharing as both a cost-saving and environmental strategy has inspired groups of people (usually from 7 to 15) to share a van for their daily commute. A designated driver rides for free and everyone else shares the costs. To simplify the process, some rental car and leasing companies are contributing. In California, Enterprise Rent-A-Car offers a vanpooling rental program. For about $75 to $120 each per month, Vanpoolers can use a van with insurance and maintenances fees included. And thanks to a Federal tax incentive program called Commuter Choice, those who work for a company that creates or sponsors a vanpool or ride share program can have up to $115 of their monthly paycheck applied tax-free to cover commuting costs.

Commuting by train or bus—even vanpooling—may be easy on your wallet and the environment, but the future of urban transport belongs to the bicycle. Imagine if a major urban center offered self-serve access to bicycles at rental stations placed a quarter-mile apart throughout the city limits. A roughly $45 annual subscription would allow residents to rent the bikes in half-hour increments—the first half hour would be free, of course, the second half hour would cost about $1.50 (from there prices would get progressively more expensive, to encourage sharing). Renters could ride the bikes wherever they wanted and then drop them off at any rental station of their choosing. Another bike would always available when they were ready to ride again. In this fantastical bicycle world, riders would never have to worry about storage or theft, since there would always be a bike station nearby. And purchasing a bicycle would be unnecessary, because bikes would be plentiful and available at any time. In this mystical metropolis, biking would give commuters a daily dose of exercise, trimming their waistlines as well as their eco-impact. And the city would reduce its air pollution and traffic congestion making life that much more pleasant for all of its fit inhabitants. The good news is that this two-wheeled utopia exists. The bad news is that it's in France. In 2007, a highly successful bicycle-share program called Velib was launched in Paris. Today, 20,000 bicycles are available for rent at 1,500 bike stations throughout the city. Lyon, France's second city, has had a successful self-service public bicycle rental program in place since 2005, and similar programs are operating throughout Europe in Barcelona, Brussels, Copenhagen, Stockholm, and Vienna.

The United States is trying to catch up—the first self-service public bicycle rental program launched in Washington, D.C., in 2008. While more modest in scale, with just 120 bicycles available at 10 stations throughout the city's central business district, SmartBike DC is a step in a smart green direction. A $40 annual fee gets you a membership card that is used to access bikes at any rental station. You can return your ride to the same station or drop it off at another location.

Other cities are becoming increasingly bike-friendly by converting old rail tracks to bikeways, establishing designated bicycling lanes on roads and instituting no-car zones. In fact, along the East Coast, a 3,000-mile-long bicycle trail aptly dubbed the East Coast Greenway is being built as a continuous bicycling path from Maine to Florida thanks to the coordination and cooperation of hundreds of local towns and cities. If all this bike talk has you feeling excited about the future yet unsure whether the average Nascar-loving American will be able to comfortably embrace this kind of change, remember that Lance Armstrong is every bit as American as Kyle Busch or Jeff Gordon. Some would even argue that he's won more championships.

Car Makes and Models

APTERA
Aptera.com
The Aptera Typ-1 electric-powered three-wheeler will redefine your expectations of what an automobile can look like. With an egg-shaped body, funky dashboard, built-in rooftop solar panels, and front wheel spokes that protrude from the body (for stability), the Typ-1 conjures images of lunar explorations. The all-electric version gets 120 miles per charge. A plug-in hybrid electric model (PHEV) ramps that closer to a mind-bending 300 miles per gallon. The starting sticker price is around $27,000.

FORD ESCAPE HYBRID SUV
Fordvehicles.com / suvs / escapehybrid / index.asp
The Ford Escape Hybrid SUV (starting msrp: $26,505; combined mpg: 32) lets you enjoy the practicality, utility, and roomy cargo space of an SUV while achieving fuel economy figures that save big at the pump and garner nods of approval from other eco-minded road warriors.

HONDA CIVIC HYBRID
Automobiles.honda.com / civic-hybrid
The stylish four-door sedan is a step up from earlier versions of the Civic. The hybrid model (starting msrp: $22,600; combined mpg: 42) comes with improved interior styling. This eco-friendly ride performs well on the outside, inside, and under the hood.

HONDA FIT
Automobiles.honda.com / fit
Slick design and multiple internal configuration possibilities make this five-door and five-seat hatchback an ideal road trip vehicle. The Fit (starting msrp: $13,950; combined mpg: 31) is designed to fit your active lifestyle. Flip the backseats down or upright to stow a bike or throw the front passenger seat all the way back for a power nap and still have space in the rear for the rest of your gear.

HONDA INSIGHT
Automobiles.honda.com / insight-hybrid
New to the market for 2009 is Honda's attempt to unseat the Toyota Prius as the most popular hybrid on the road today. The Honda Insight is a five-door hatchback that is expected to achieve combined gas mileage of over 40 mpg and cost around $19,000, making it the most affordable hybrid available.

MINI CLUBMAN
Miniusa.com
Pick your colors, slap on the racing stripes, and hit the accelerator. You're going to love the improved ride and versatility of this second generation stretched MINI (starting msrp: $19,950; combined mpg: 32). The look-at-me design is as eccentric as it is appealing.

NISSAN ALTIMA HYBRID
Nissanusa.com/altima
The large gas tank of the Altima Hybrid (starting msrp: $25,170; combined mpg: 34) lets you go for nearly 600 miles before you ever have to make a pit stop at the gas station, which is fantastic for your wallet but might not be so wonderful for your bladder.

SMART FORTWO
Smartusa.com
The Smart ForTwo (starting msrp: $11,590; combined mpg: 36) is a stylish two-seater that is surprisingly roomy on the inside while narrow enough on the outside to go head-first into parking spaces.

TH!NK CITY
Think.no
The TH!NK *city* electric-powered car considers your wallet (you can own one starting at around $25,000) and your style (the streamlined design features side indicator lights, strong wheel arches, and a variety of striking colors), without forsaking the environment. With a top speed of 65 miles per hour and a 110-mile range per charge, it's an excellent choice for commuters seeking to break their addiction to gasoline.

TOYOTA CAMRY HYBRID
Toyota.com/camry
The most popular car in America comes in a fuel-efficient hybrid version. The Camry Hybrid (starting msrp: $25,350; combined mpg: 34) enables you to conserve gas and do your bit for the environment without drawing attention to yourself. It's the car of choice for those who are concerned about the environment but harbor suspicions that environmentalism is still somehow vaguely Communist.

TOYOTA PRIUS
Toyota.com/prius-hybrid
The belle of the hybrid ball, the Prius (starting msrp: $21,500; combined mpg: 46) delivers the highest fuel mileage ratings of any fuel-powered car on the road. It's also the car model of choice for Lazy Environmentalists who want

to broadcast their eco-credentials. You will never see a bumper sticker on a Prius—the Prius *is* the bumper sticker.

TOYOTA YARIS

Toyota.com / Yaris

The Yaris (starting msrp: $11,350; combined mpg: 32) is available in both three-door hatchback and four-door sedan models. Hipsters will undoubtedly veer toward the three-door version for the simple reason that it totally rocks.

VOLKSWAGEN JETTA

Vw.com / jetta

New and improved diesel-engine cars are back, and the most affordable and fun to drive is the Volkswagen Jetta TDI. Choose either the four-door sedan (starting msrp: $22,640; combined mpg: 34) or the SportWagen (starting msrp: $23,590; combined mpg: 34). Both combine turbocharged high-performance with crisp power-assisted rack-and-pinion steering.

Motor Scooter Makes and Models

APRILIA SCARABEO

Apriliausa.com

Aprilia's line of Scarabeo motor scooters traces its Italian heritage back to the post-WWII era and the region of Venice. The Scarabeo 200 is a superbly crafted urban commuter that tops out near 80 mph and a delivers a whopping 70 mpg. Its large 16-inch wheels provide stability and a sense of overall safety. At $3,399 it truly combines performance and affordability.

HONDA METROPOLITAN

Powersports.honda.com / scooters

Enjoy the classic retro styling of Honda's Metropolitan 49cc motor scooter, which puts the fun back in commuting and running errands. With a top speed of 35 mph, fuel economy of around 80 mpg, and a sticker price of $2,049, the eco-savvy Metropolitan will put a smile on your face and leave some cash in your pocket.

KYMCO PEOPLE

Strmotorsports.com

Kymco offers several motor scooter brands, but it's the company's People line that really turns heads with its modern styling, big wheels, and funky color combinations. The People 150 is priced right at $2,799 and will deliver a top speed of 65 mph and about 70 mpg.

PIAGGIO FLY

Piaggiousa.com

The parent company of such illustrious Italian motorcycle and motor scooter brands like Moto Guzzi, Gilera, Derbi, Vespa, and Aprilia, Piaggio also offers its own brand of affordable, stylish motor scooters. The Fly 50 ($1,899) and 150 ($2,899) are reliable and affordable machines that deliver solid performance.

VEKEN HYBRID

Vekenscooters.com

A newcomer to the motor scooter scene, Veken elevates fuel efficiency to new levels with the Veken Hybrid VK-M50, a combination gas and electric hybrid scooter capable of achieving 212 mpg. The lithium-ion battery charges automatically while you ride it, but you can also recharge it on your own by plugging the scooter into any outlet. The price tag is $2,799, and the scooter can go up to 35 mph.

VESPA LX

Vespausa.com

Famous for their exceptional quality, and iconic Italian design, Vespa motor scooters are available through a broad dealership network throughout the United States. Vespas retain their market exceptionally well over time because they're made with the finest parts, including a solid stainless steel frame. At $3,299, the Vespa LX is the most affordable model and delivers around 70 mpg.

YAMAHA VINO

Yamaha-motor.com/sport

For a high-quality ride with retro flair and an even more affordable price point, check out the Yamaha Vino. The Vino 125 sells for $2,899 and averages 96 mpg. The four-stroke engine delivers a top speed of around 55 mph. The Vino Classic is an entry-level 49cc scooter that sells for $2,049, delivers 112 mpg, and has a maximum speed of 35 miles mph.

ZERO X

Zeromotorcycles.com

Go from zero to 30 mph in just two seconds on the Zero X off-road electric motorcycle. The battery pack delivers about 40 miles per charge and a top speed of just below 60 miles per hour. The standard model costs $7,450, and long-term savings are guaranteed since plugging into the power grid only takes two hours and costs about a penny per mile. Look for the Zero S, a street-legal electric motorcycle that's in development.

Car Share, Ride Share, and Vanpool Services

ENTERPRISE RENT-A-CAR RIDESHARE
Vanpool.com
Enterprise is about more than just car rentals. The company's Vanpool service makes it easy for commuters throughout California to set up their vanpool for about $75 to $120 per month per person including insurance and maintenances fees.

GOLOCO.ORG
Share rides to work, concerts, sporting events, or even the farmers' market using GoLoco. The company's website utilizes Facebook's social networking platform, enabling users to create personal profiles and choose compatible riding companions. The website also handles all financial transactions to remove the awkwardness of requesting gas and toll money from fellow travelers.

NURIDE
Nuride.com
Nuride is an online ride sharing service with more than 28,000 members who receive reward points for sharing rides. The service operates just like an airline membership rewards program. The more rides you share, the more points you earn and the more value you can redeem. Partners include Applebee's, Austin Grill, Dunkin' Donuts, and Ringling Brothers and Barnum & Bailey Circus.

PICKUPPAL
Pickuppal.com
Combine your ride sharing trips with package delivery to earn a little extra cash on the way. PickUpPal connects drivers, passengers, and packages heading in the same direction to consolidate trips and thus lower carbon greenhouse gas emissions. Available in locations throughout the world, PickupPal is also the ride sharing partner of the London Symphony Orchestra.

RIDE AMIGOS
Rideamigos.com
Connect with people going your way to share a taxicab or a car anywhere on Earth. Ride Amigos helps you lower your costs while conveniently getting you to your destination. Companys can use the service to help fellow employees coordinate trips together.

SHARELING

Shareling.com

Connect with fellow travelers looking to share a road trip using Shareling's interactive maps that show available rides around the globe. It's the budget- and planet-friendly way to travel across Europe or to catch all the fresh snow powder runs between Banff in the Canadian Rockies and Taos in New Mexico.

VPSI

Vanpoolusa.com

The largest provider of commuter vanpool services in the United States, VPSI maintains a fleet of nearly 4,000 vans that help commuters lower their costs and environmental impact and travel to work in stress-free style. Visit the website to find vanpools in your area.

WECAR

Wecar.com

Rental car giant Enterprise-Rent-A-Car has partnered with the city of St. Louis, Missouri, to introduce its WeCar car share service. Members can take advantage of an all-hybrid fleet of cars parked at convenient locations throughout the downtown area.

ZIMRIDE

Zimride.com

Zimride is a ride share service built on a social networking platform enabling members to create personal profiles and select ride mates who share similar music tastes, favorite sports teams, or who just seem "normal." Zimmers can also evaluate things like driving speed, music volume, and smoking preferences before agreeing to hop in. Find rides at Zimride.com or by using Zimride's Facebook application, which makes the service available to Facebook's 80 million users.

ZIPCAR

Zipcar.com

Zipcar is like, "Hey Dad, can I borrow your car tonight?" without having to ask your dad. This car-share service is perfect for people who normally use public transportation but need a vehicle for a couple of hours or a day for a doctor's appointment, beach excursion, or a night on the town. Membership is minimal and the cars are new, stylish, and available in cities all over the country.

Ones to Watch

CHEVY VOLT PHEV

If General Motors can successfully deliver the Chevy Volt plug-in hybrid electric vehicle (PHEV) to market, the world might never look the same again. That's because the Volt is one of the most stylish green cars in development and is potentially capable of achieving 360 mpg. The price tag for this green game changer is still uncertain, but GM hopes to offer it for around $30,000. Look for the Volt starting in 2010.

HYBRID TRAVELERS

Hybridtravelers.com

Hybrid car owners are eligible for lower car insurance rates thanks to a discount program offered by Hybrid Travelers. Because hybrid owners tend to be lower risk drivers, Travelers rewards them with a 10 percent discount on premiums.

PROGRESSIVE AUTOMOTIVE X PRIZE

Progressiveautoxprize.org

This competition, with $10 million on the line, is intended to make superefficient, 100 mpg cars a reality for consumers sooner rather than later. Teams from around the world develop cars that will compete in a cross-country road rally in the United States beginning in late 2009. The team with the best cumulative fuel efficiency and fastest time through the multiple stages wins. To date, 94 teams from 14 countries have signed up to go for the glory.

PROJECT BETTER PLACE

Projectbetterplace.com

To speed along the widespread use of electric cars, Project Better Place is creating a network of battery charging and exchange stations to give electric car drivers easy access to electricity in lieu of gasoline. Israel and Denmark have already signed on with the company to shift their countries toward a cleaner transportation future. And Renault-Nissan is already working on developing electric cars.

SMARTBIKE DC

Smartbikedc.com

In 2008, Washington, D.C., launched the first self-service public bicycle rental program in the country. While initially modest in scale, with just 120 bicycles available at 10 stations throughout the city's central business district,

SmartBike DC is a step in a smart green direction. A $40 annual fee gets you a membership card that is used to access bikes at any rental station.

Information/Resources

AUTOBLOGGREEN.COM
Monitor the latest green automotive developments at this blog dedicated to keeping its readers current with rapid industry innovation. If it's got wheels and an engine and is helping to reduce global greenhouse gas emissions, you can likely read about it here.

BUILD YOUR OWN ELECTRIC VEHICLE
Mcgraw-hillnursing.com/product.php?isbn=0071543732
DIYers will appreciate this book by Seth Leitman and Bob Brant, which shows you everything you need to know to transform your own gas-powered car into an a clean, zero-emission electric vehicle. Instead of waiting around for the electric car revolution to materialize, you can realize the benefits today by doing it yourself.

CARSHARING.NET
A comprehensive resource for learning about the benefits of car share programs, Carsharing.net also lists car-share programs available in cities throughout North America, Europe, Asia, and Australia and New Zealand.

COMMUTER CHOICE
Commuterchoice.com
Commuter Choice is a federal tax incentive program that enables people to have up to $115 of their monthly paycheck applied tax-free to cover commuting costs. The program is only available to employees whose employers participate in the program. Fortunately, any company can sign up. If you bike, skate, or walk to work, take public transit, or belong to a vanpool or carpool, then you are eligible.

CYCLECHIC
Cyclechic.co.uk
Bicycling is a very cool planetary solution for getting around, but if you're in need of some fashion cues on how to do it style check out this guide to urban cycling fashion. The trendy site has been featured in the likes of *Vogue* attesting to just how fashionable it's becoming to ride with two wheels instead of four.

FUELECONOMY.GOV

Get gas mileage tips, learn about energy-efficient vehicles, and compare cars for greenhouse gas emissions, air pollution, and miles per gallon at this site sponsored by the EPA's Department of Energy Efficiency and Renewable Energy.

THE LAZY ENVIRONMENTALIST

Lazyenvironmentalist.com/transportation

I've created a special page to keep Lazy Environmentalist readers updated about ongoing developments in eco-friendly transportation. Get the latest scoop on eco-friendly cars and motor scooters and learn about innovative ways to green your ride.

GREEN CAR JOURNAL

Greencar.com

A terrific resource for learning about specific car models, technologies, and trends impacting green automobile transportation. Articles are well-written, informative, and are geared toward consumers who want to learn about their eco-options but who aren't schooled in automotive industry jargon.

HYBRIDCARS.COM

Bradley Berman and company are the go-to team for all things hybrid. His site has information on every aspect of hybrid cars, from gas mileage and oil dependency to cultural impact and environmental benefits.

4

Cool Ways to Conserve Energy

Wouldn't it be awesome if your home generated

all of its own power, freeing you from rising energy rates and allowing you to live comfortably while treading lightly on the planet? Though recent advancements in clean energy are bringing this eco-utopian dream closer to reality, cost is, unfortunately, still a major factor. But all hope is not lost for the Lazy Environmentalist on a budget. There are simple steps you can take to dramatically reduce your energy output while saving money. Since the EPA estimates that the average household spends more than $2,000 per year on energy and historical trends point to a steady increase in prices for all residential power sources—electric, propane, natural gas, and kerosene—implementing easy energy-saving measures is in nothing but our enlightened self-interest.

SET THE RIGHT TEMPERATURE

Until recently most homes in the United States were built under the assumption that energy is cheap and abundant. This may explain why the EPA has found that the average household spends about $1,000 every year, or 50 percent of its total energy consumption, seeking the perfect indoor temperature. Building houses capable of capitalizing on the natural heat and light from the sun or cooling from tree shade and breezes was rarely done. As a result, we've got some pretty dumb houses. To counter your home's deficient IQ, start by installing a digital, programmable thermostat that lets you automatically control and adjust your home's temperature throughout the day. Good ones range in price from $35 to $80 and can reduce your heating and cooling costs by about 20 percent per year. Of course, to reap those benefits you have to take the time to program them, which is why Energy Star requires that all of its qualified models come with four pre-programmed settings to automatically adjust temperatures throughout the night and day—an ideal situation for Lazy Environmentalists. If you're feeling ambitious, you can always override the settings to suit your particular needs. Lux makes several affordable models that are highly rated by *Consumer Reports* for ease of programming, temperature accuracy, and clear display. They start at around $35 and are available at numerous retailers, including Ace Hardware. The Honeywell FocusPro 6000 series ($70) is equipped with an easy-to-read display and is compatible with central air conditioning units as well as electric, gas, or oil furnaces and heat pumps. Unless you're adept at home remodeling projects, you may wish to have a local HVAC (heating, ventilating, and air conditioning) professional install your model.

For those who survive the sweltering season with individual air conditioner units, a digital thermostat won't be much help. The best way to stay cool, use less energy, and reduce your bills is to choose Energy Star–rated models that have an EER (Energy Efficient Ratio) over 10. EER measures the ratio of cooling capacity to energy usage, and top-notch Energy Star models sometimes go to 11. Look for affordable, top-rated models from GE, Frigidaire, Haier, and Kenmore. See Greenerchoices.com, a website run by Consumers Union, the nonprofit publisher of *Consumer Reports,* for a list of best buys. But while looking for the ultimate AC, don't forget the ceiling fans. Fans are easy to install and a cost-effective method of cooling your home while creating a feeling of tropical relaxation. Visit Energystar.gov to search for models that consume less energy.

GREEN THE FRIDGE

Next to heating and cooling, running the refrigerator is the second most energy-intensive residential activity. Refrigerators account for 14 percent of all energy use for the average household. Switching to an energy-efficient model can save you a bundle, with current Energy Star models clocking in at least 40 percent more energy efficient than refrigerators built before 2001. For the budget-minded, top-freezer models are usually the way to go since they offer the most storage at the most affordable price. The Frigidaire FRT18S6AW is a top-freezer unit (about $550) that's a great choice for smaller apartments thanks to a slim profile that offers 18 cubic feet of storage space. While the fridge comes with few bells and whistles, it gets the job done with plenty of room for veggies, beer, and leftovers. One of the most highly rated top-freezer refrigerators is the Whirlpool ET1FHTXM (about $850), with about 21 cubic feet of storage room. Nice perks include an interior ice maker, water dispenser, spill-control glass shelves, and gallon storage on the door. To get the skinny on a wide range of quality, energy-efficient refrigerators, check out Greenerchoices.org.

CHOOSE ENERGY-SMART ELECTRONICS

We Americans like our TV. Yes we do. We enjoy it so much that the EPA and Department of Energy now estimate that televisions in combination with related products like set-top boxes (the device that connects your TV to an external digital television signal) and DVD players account for 10 percent of the average household's energy use, and that number is rising. As for energy efficiency, conventional wisdom holds that when it comes to flat-panel models, those with LCD (liquid crystal display) screens are more efficient than their plasma screen counterparts. This is mostly true, but since energy output depends upon the specific model you choose, your best bet is to visit Energystar.gov and check for TV models that meet the new, stricter Energy Star standards, which went into effect in November 2008. When you choose an Energy Star–qualified TV, you're choosing a device that uses significantly less energy than its conventional counterpart when it's turned on *and* when it's off. Sound strange? Blame it on the "vampire" effect. One of the pitfalls of modern living is that everything we leave plugged into the electric socket uses energy even when turned off—some estimates have found that 5 percent of all energy in the country (and of every household) is wasted as result of this power-sucking phenomenon. Unless you plan to unplug your television and all other electronics when they're not in use, you can achieve savings of about 30 percent by selecting Energy Star products that use less energy whether they're turned on or off.

You can also combat vampire energy drain the super lazy way by plugging your television and all related devices into a Smart Strip Power Strip. Available online for under $40 at numerous outlets like Smarthomeusa.com, the Smart Strip comes with 10 outlets: one blue, six white, and three red. When you plug your television into the main outlet (the blue one), all devices plugged into the white outlets become connected to its on/off status. So when you turn your TV on, all the other devices automatically turn on. When you turn your TV off, all the other devices automatically shut off. The three red outlets enable you to operate devices— like lava lamps and curling irons—independently of the TV's on/ off status. And because the Smart Strip Power Strip is just that, it senses when devices are turned off and cuts all power to those devices, eliminating the dreaded vampire effect. The strip performs equally as well when operating with computers and their related peripherals (printers, scanners, speakers, etc.) and is an excellent power surge protector. A smaller, 7-outlet version is also available for around $30.

When looking for the latest in eco-savvy flat screen TVs, start with Phillips Eco LCD HDTV line. Media technology site CNET. com found that the 42-inch (model# 42PFL5603D) is the only flat-panel HDTV with a screen size of 27 inches or greater that delivers an excellent picture while using less than 100 watts of energy—91.23 to be exact, less than a 100-watt incandescent light bulb. When resting in standby mode the TV sips a miserly .73 watts. Models tested from other well-known brands used up to two to three times that amount. At about $1,200, it's not exactly a steal, but it is priced competitively with other high-quality LCD models. You can purchase Phillips 42-inch Eco TVs at Amazon.com as well as other online retailers like Buy.com and Dell.com. The line also includes a 32-inch, 47-inch, and 52-inch model.

To outfit your home with the finest planet-protecting home electronics and computers start with reliable Energystar.gov. You'll find Energy Star–rated models for cordless phones, DVD players, printers, audio tuners, and more. Greenerchoices.org also ranks numerous computer models based on their performance and energy efficiency. Dell, HP, Lenovo, Sony, and Apple offer machines that rank well at affordable prices. You can also check out the best in eco-computers at Epeat.net, the online home of the Electronic Product Environmental Assessment Tool, a program from the Green Electronics Council. As of this writing the Gold standard categories in desktops, laptops, and monitors are dominated by Dell, HP, Lenovo, and Toshiba. However, even with the most energy-efficient computers, the simplest way to conserve energy is to shut them down or set them to automatically switch into sleep mode when not in use.

CONSIDER THE WATER HEATER

Ranking fourth on our list of greatest energy used in the home is water heating, coming in at about 9 percent of total household power. Factoring in installation costs, heaters of all varieties, from storage boilers to tankless water heaters, can get pricey pretty quickly with costs hovering around $800 or beyond. Energy Star—rated models only promise minimal gains in energy efficiency—around a 6 percent improvement. But since water heating for the average household costs nearly $200 per year, several quick, affordable measures will yield benefits. First, install low-flow showerheads. They greatly reduce the amount of hot water you'll need in the first place, which means your water heater won't have to work as hard (see Chapter 5: Eco-H2O for details on specific products). Second, lower the water heater temperature on your heater's thermostat. In most cases, adjusting the thermostat down to 120°F will provide ample hot water for all household tasks. And each 10°F reduction in temperature will lower your water heating costs by 3 to 5 percent. Since the typical temperature setting for most hot water heaters is 180°F, you may be able to save 18–30 percent on your water heating costs without springing for a new model. Another trick is to insulate the hot and cold water pipes that connect to your heater (this will bring about only minimal savings). Wrapping your water-storage tank in insulation also helps to prevent

Scott Clark is co-founder and CEO of Appalachian Energy, a company that provides renewable energy solutions to businesses and residents.

How did you get the idea for Appalachian Energy?

Appalachian Energy was the result of my father's experience in the nuclear and hydroelectric industry while living in Canada. He has always had a strong passion for the energy and HVAC sectors, and when he moved to Asheville, North Carolina, in 1996 it was his goal to return to the energy industry with a focus on renewable energy. On December 31, 2003, Appalachian Energy began producing real renewable energy at our 1.2 MW hydroelectric facility on the Ivy River in Madison County, North Carolina. The founding members were my father, our good friend Wesley Dodge, and me. We're three guys who share a very strong passion for a clean and energy-efficient future.

What is Appalachian Energy's positive environmental impact?

We begin by educating homeowners about how their annual energy bill relates to their specific energy usage. Once that's clear, then we develop solutions that will get the biggest bang (energy savings) for the buck. For example, the average family in North Carolina spends $2,800 per year on energy, 40 percent of which is for hot water and space heating. To help alleviate these costs, we frequently recommend our solar hot water and heating systems. After federal and state incentives, the average system costs about $6,000 and will conservatively save about $800 a year. Looking at this strictly from an investment standpoint, that's a 13.3 percent annual return—pretty good. From an environmental standpoint, it's the equivalent of eliminating 1 to 3 metric tons of greenhouse gas emissions (depending upon whether your current heating system uses oil, natural gas, propane, or electric). That's the equivalent of eliminating 1.7 to 2.5 barrels of oil per person/per year or not driving a car for 6 months (based on average 12,000 miles per year). When you know the problem, you can find the solution and without a doubt have a positive impact.

If I live alone should I take extra-long showers to reap the full benefits of my system? Or should I invite friends over to shower at my place too?

We suggest showering long enough to get clean. Remember, the system will also help heat water for other major uses like running the dishwasher and the clothes washer. As for your friends, I'd really have to meet them first to gauge whether or not it's a good idea to invite them over.

unnecessary heat loss, but most tanks have already been insulated by the manufacturer. A quick touch test will tell you if your heater can benefit from an insulation blanket. If it's hot consider insulation, which will only require $25 and a quick visit to Home Depot or Lowe's. If it's cool, your heater is already doing its job efficiently.

OPTIMIZE YOUR LIGHTING

Lighting comes in at number five on the home energy charts, at roughly less than 9 percent of all energy use, right behind hot water heating. Illuminating all those lightbulbs costs nearly $200 per year for the average household. The most affordable way to bring these costs down, assuming you've already raised the widow blinds to allow natural light to shine through, is to switch from incandescent bulbs to compact fluorescent bulbs (CFLs). Recent technological improvements are helping CFLs surpass the incandescent competition. On top of that, they use one-fourth the energy of incandescents to produce the same amount of light while lasting 10 times longer. In 2007, *Popular Mechanics Magazine* put seven brands of CFLs to the test and found that they all produced better lighting quality than their incandescent bulb counterparts. The judges included three *Popular Mechanics* staffers as well as a lighting expert from the Parsons School of Design in New York City. Currently, CFLs still carry a cost premium over incandescent bulbs, but not for long. The average household has about forty-five lightbulbs, and if you were to exchange those bulbs for CFLs you'd save about

$150 annually on your energy bill for the next 10 years. How much would it cost to make the switch? Head to Home Depot and pick up a two-pack of the top-rated n:vision "soft white" or "bright white" CFLs for $6.88, or $3.44 per bulb, available in 75-watt or 100-watt equivalents. At $3.44 per bulb, you'd pay $158.24 for 46 bulbs, enough to change your entire house and have one spare remaining. Essentially, what you pay up front is equal to what you save in year one and every year afterward. Another option is to visit Environmentalhomecenter.com, the website for a growing chain of green home supply stores throughout the northwestern United States, and take advantage of the 99-cent deal on Durabright 75-watt equivalent CFLs. Forty-five of them will run you about $45. There's also Wal-Mart, where a broad selection of GE CFLs can be purchased in bulk to obtain major discounts—a 6-pack of 75- or 100-watt equivalent CFLs is available for $19.32, or $3.22 per bulb.

There is, however, a dirty little secret about CFLs: Sealed safely within their glass tubing is a tiny amount of mercury. Should a CFL break inside your home, it's recommended that you open the windows and use gloves to clean up the mess. Put the broken pieces in a glass jar, seal it, and visit Earth911.org to find a local recycling center where the bulb can be properly disposed of. Getting acquainted with your local recycling center is important anyway, since you'll either bring your used CFLs there or to your nearest Home Depot. In 2008, the nation's second-largest retailer introduced a used CFL recycling program available at all of its stores.

Another way to conserve energy—and money—is to install lighting occupancy sensors inside your home (an excellent trick for forgetful environmentalists). You know how sometimes you pull into a friend's driveway and the light goes on above the garage? Then, assuming your friend lets you in, the light shuts off after a few minutes? These lights rely upon a motion detector to turn them on and off. The same principle can be applied inside your home to turn lights on when you enter a room and turn them off after a short delay when you leave. Watt Stopper makes a range of lighting occupancy sensors that sell for around $40. They're installed directly in wall switchplates and give you the option to manually override the motion sensor and switch lights on and off yourself should you so desire. Watt Stopper sensors are compatible with CFL bulbs—just think of all the savings! Get the sensors, reduce energy use, and save money.

If you prefer to be flooded with natural light from dawn to dusk, then you will go absolutely gaga for tubular skylights. Unlike conventional skylights, which are really just a big window in the ceiling, tubular skylights emit light like regular ceiling fixtures do except the source of the light isn't electricity but rather the sun's rays. Sunshine is channeled from your rooftop through a narrow tube (that runs through your walls and floorboards) down into your living space. Solatube is one of the leadings brands in the industry. Its tubes can fit easily between roof rafters and require no structural changes to install. They can extend as long as 30 feet and are lined with highly reflective mirrors that funnel light down the shaft. A 10-inch tube and ceiling fixture costs about $300 and is perfect for lighting smaller spaces like bathrooms, laundry rooms, and hallways. The 14-inch model costs about $425 and is great for larger areas like kitchens or living rooms. Daylight dimmer switches (they can be added for about $60) give you complete control of your sunlight. For about $50 a CFL socket can also be installed inside the ceiling fixture for nighttime lighting. Because these tubular skylights are effective even when it's cloudy, you may never again have to turn the lights on during the day.

AUDIT YOUR ENERGY USE

In addition to implementing these specific measures, you can always call upon a professional to give your home a comprehensive energy audit. Home Energy Auditors (or Raters as they are sometimes called) check for drafts that may be allowing heated or cooled air to escape from any number of places in your home, including windows, doors, baseboard moldings, fireplace dampers, attic access hatches, and plumbing and wiring penetrations in floors, ceilings, and walls to name some of the most common trouble spots. They'll also check to see whether your home is properly insulated and evaluate the efficiency of your systems, appliances, and electronics. Some will troubleshoot problems as they go. Others will generate a list of specific cost-effective improvements. To find an energy auditor, first check with your local utility (they will usually provide a basic energy audit for free). Energystar.gov also maintains a database of certified Home Energy Raters who can evaluate a home's energy efficiency and offer recommendations. And RESNET (Residential Energy Services Network) is another national organization that certifies energy auditors. Auditors will rank your home on a scale of 1 to 100 (1 is the most efficient) and generate a list of recommended measures. The ratings can also help you qualify for energy-efficient mortgages, federal tax credits, and become registered as an Energy Star–certified home. Improving the energy efficiency of your home saves you money on your energy bills, and it also increases the real estate value of your home. This means that doing what's best for the planet will not only save you money today but will lead to a bigger payday in the future.

CASH IN ON REBATES AND INCENTIVES

Government agencies and institutions at the local, state, and federal level are pitching in to further incentivize all of us to conserve energy (and upgrade our lifestyles). Before purchasing new systems, appliances, electronics, or lighting for your home, check the websites of your local government and power utility to see whether incentives are available. Residents living in the northeastern United States can visit Myenergystar.com to scan a database of instant coupons and rebates provided by local power utilities. Deals may include receiving $2 off of CFLs that cost more than $2.50 or receiving $30 to $40 off the purchase of a new room air conditioner. DSIRE (Database of State Incentives for Renewables and Efficiency) maintains a comprehensive database of state, local, utility, and federal incentives to encourage energy efficiency and the adoption of renewable energy. They're usually in the form of rebates, tax credits, and favorable financing rates for energy-efficiency improvements.

EMBRACE RENEWABLE ENERGY

A quick Lazy Environmentalist calculation finds that residential renewable energy has never made much economic sense. Try as some might to convince us that we're really "saving" money when we outlay thousands of dollars on a residential solar or wind energy system, it's natural to resist plopping down a huge chunk of change for clean energy when we can still easily get our power on the cheap from the local utility. Sure, installing solar panels or residential wind turbines lowers—or altogether eliminates—our home's energy bills and greenhouse gas emissions, increases our real estate property value, and improves air quality. And yes, clean energy sources enhance our national security and economic well-being by ensuring that a sufficient power supply is available to meet our nation's growing needs. Yet, the financial commitment has still been difficult to stomach. But things are looking up.

TAP THE SUN

Technological improvements, savvier green businesses, and rising energy rates are shifting the residential renewable energy landscape. And California is leading the way. The state's tiered price structure for energy usage imposes higher energy rates on homeowners when they use more energy. According to the U.S. Department of Energy, the average U.S. household uses 888 kilowatt hours (kWh) of energy per month and pays just over 10 cents per kWh. In California, the nearly 5 million residents who get their energy from Pacific Gas & Electric (PG&E), the state's largest utility company, pay about 11 cents per kWh for the first 480 kWh of energy used. The rate then kicks up to a reasonably affordable rate of about 13 cents for energy between 481 kWh and 625 kWh. Then it spikes to about 23 cents per kWh for energy between 626 kWh and 960 kWh. The top rate is close to 37 cents for energy over 1440 kWh per month. The cost structure clearly encourages homeowners to conserve energy. It also makes solar power a cost-competitive option for those paying 37 cents or even 23 cents per kWh for a major chunk of their energy usage. This is where next-generation green entrepreneurs enter the picture.

If somebody were to offer me a way to power my home with solar energy without paying any money up front, I'd listen. That somebody is SolarCity. In 2008, SolarCity introduced SolarLease, a program that enables homeowners to lease solar panel systems for a low monthly rate and zero money down. SolarCity even provides free repair service and free monitoring for optimal output as part of the performance guarantee, which lasts as long as the lease. Leases run for 15 years, after which time you can apply your accumulated monthly payments toward purchasing your system or opt to return it back to the company. Along the way, you'll very likely lower your overall monthly energy costs. SolarCity doesn't normally recommend installing systems that provide 100 percent of a home's energy needs. Instead, the company's technicians recommend systems that eliminate the money spent on energy at the higher rates charged by California's utility companies. You still use just enough utility-provided energy to take advantage of the low rates, but now clean, emissions-free solar power covers the rest. This works for your bottom line and the planet's too.

Another way to make solar energy more affordable is to eliminate the high costs of installation. Here's a little-known fact: When you purchase a solar power system for your home, typically only 50 percent of the up front cost is for the solar panels. The other 50 percent pays for the labor and equipment necessary to install the system. That's why ReadySolar developed a deceptively simple modular system, aptly named Solar in a Box, that can be installed quickly and at a reduced cost. The plug-and-play system removes much of the complexity surrounding solar panel installation and makes it easy for technicians trained on the system to install them in half the time of traditional systems. Because Solar in a Box is a modular system, you can choose as little or as much solar power as you'd like and then add more capacity over time. The sleek, modular panel systems lay flat to the roof and are designed to integrate into the overall aesthetic design of your house. You get the benefits of a clean energy source, but unless you feel like boasting, your neighbors may not even notice that they're there.

Other companies are working to make financing for solar power systems more affordable and accessible. Clean Power Finance is developing relationships with banks across the United States and creating relationships with solar installers to facilitate access to low-rate loans for solar panel systems. Operating throughout the Northeast, Northwest, and Canada, GroSolar is steadily becoming one of the largest solar installers in North America. Where rebates and incentives are available in your state, GroSolar files all of the paperwork on your behalf. And since rebate checks can take a while to arrive, GroSolar charges you the "after rebate" price when installing your system and then collects the incentive checks directly, helping to lower your out-of-pocket costs. In states like New York and New Jersey, where rebates can equal 50 percent or more of a solar system, we're talking about thousands of dollars that you don't have to lay out.

One solar company is collaborating directly with a financing company to help make your sun-powered dreams a reality. Akeena Solar has developed a sleek, easy-to-install solar panel system called Andalay and has partnered with an innovative solar financing company called Sun Run to help consumers go solar without incurring much of the up front costs. Sun Run enables residents to enter into a long-term contract called a Power Purchase Agreement (PPA), which helps a homeowner purchase the energy being produced by the solar panels on the roof without actually purchasing or leasing the panels. Sun Run acts like your own local solar utility, essentially charging you a fixed energy rate per month for using the solar energy from your roof system. The rate is often lower than what your utility company currently charges and is locked in for the entire contract (usually 20 years) as a hedge against rising energy prices. You'll pay an up front cost of a few thousand dollars for the system, which takes about 10 years to recoup, but it's a much smaller output of cash to get the clean, green energy benefits of your own solar system.

In North Carolina, Appalachian Energy, one of the fastest-growing solar energy companies in the Southeast, is taking an alternative approach to harnessing the sun's rays and lowering your energy costs. The company's residential solar energy system uses solar thermal panels to capture the sun's heat and then uses it to help meet your home's hot water and space heating needs. Other solar thermal system companies offer solutions designed to help with hot water. But by doing double-duty as a space heating solution, Appalachian Energy's system cuts your bills by nearly twice as much as conventional solar thermal systems. Because the space heating component easily integrates into your home's current HVAC system without the need for additional expensive equipment, Appalachian Energy is able to keep prices affordable. Here's the math: A system that would meet 85 percent of the average home's hot water needs and 30 percent of its space heating needs costs about $11,000. A federal incentive program knocks $2,000 off the price. A North Carolina incentive program reduces that number by an additional $3,400. If you live in the Tar Heel state, the system will run you a mere $5,600. The company estimates that such a system can save the average homeowner between $800 and $1,000 per year on energy costs. Tally it all up, and it's clear that this relatively small solar investment pays for itself pretty quickly.

RIDE THE WIND

Wind energy is beautiful. Wind energy is beautiful. Wind energy is beautiful. If all Americans would just repeat that mantra every morning upon waking, we could easily solve global warming. According to the U.S. Department of Energy, there is enough wind energy potential in the country to meet 100 percent of the country's electricity needs. And these days residential wind turbines come in multiple shapes and sizes designed to meet your personal aesthetic, power, and budget preferences. The day is soon coming when baseball, apple pie, and wind turbines will be the symbols of the American way of life.

The big windmill on the residential block is the Skystream 3.7 from Southwest Wind Energy. The Skystream is a sleek, stylized, scaled-down version of the massive wind turbines now used in wind farms. Its "plug and play" capability enables quick installation to begin converting wind into electricity for your home. The Skystream can generate anywhere from 40 to 100 percent of a home's electricity needs and costs about $5,400. Factoring in installation costs minus rebates and incentives, a fully operational unit can in many instances be yours for between $6,000 and $8,000, though prices may run as high $14,000 depending on your location. Provided your house resides on at least half an acre of unobstructed land where wind speeds average 10 miles per hour or greater, you could be a prime candidate for the Skystream (find local wind maps by state at Skystreamenergy.com). You'll also need an interconnection agreement from your utility (most offer them) and live in a community that permits structures of at least 42 feet tall. Unfortunately, the latter is not as simple as you might think.

Securing approval to install a wind turbine is rubbing up against some resistance from local zoning boards in communities throughout the United States. Though many people want to tap the clean power of the wind and the sun, local zoning boards are concerned about disruptive factors such as noise creation, endangering birds, long shadows cast onto neighbors' property, and general ugliness. As far as noise and birds go the concerns are mostly groundless. Today's best residential generators are usually quieter than the ambient outdoor sounds that are emitted from household products like air conditioners. They also pose little risk to birds due to their lower heights and smaller blades when compared to commercial wind generators. But residential wind generators do cast shadows. Yet whether they're ugly is in the eye of the beholder—though as costs continue to increase for grid energy and decrease for solar and wind energy, I suspect these generators will begin to look more attractive to everyone.

To overcome zoning restrictions, boost wind turbine efficiency, decrease costs, and provide wind energy solutions that better blend with the scale of many neighborhoods, entrepreneurs are developing vertical-axis wind turbines (VAWTs). Think of the spin of a merry-go-round—that's what the rotation of a VAWT closely resembles. The wind spins them on their vertical axis, and as they turn round and round they generate energy.

PacWind is emerging as one of the leaders in residential VAWT technology as the wind solution of choice for the likes of Jay Leno and Ed Begley Jr. PacWind turbines combine some of the most advanced technology in the field with quiet, clean designs that blend into both urban and suburban surroundings. Models of varying size, cost, and wind-generating capacity are available to meet your needs. The entry-level wind generator is the Seahawk. Retail prices start at around $3,000 for the base unit and run to $7,000 for installation, before rebates and incentives. At two and a half feet in diameter and just four feet tall, the Seahawk is a compact wind energy generator that can provide energy at winds speeds as low as 7.5 miles per hour. For a more powerful solution you'll want to check out the Delta 1, a roof-mountable wind generator that costs about $9,500 including installation before rebates and incentives. The Delta 1 could easily pass for a weathervane, yet its fast-revolving blades generate some serious wind power. At an average wind speed of 15 miles per hour, the Delta 1 will deliver more than 40 percent of the average home's electricity needs. If you live in a high wind zone, where average gusts blow at 25 miles per hour, the Delta 1 will provide enough power take you right off the power grid. How quickly this wind turbine pays you back depends on how *much* wind blows, but not on which *way* the wind blows. PacWind's turbines are omni-directional, that is, they automatically adjust to wind direction without stopping or slowing down, giving you the most bang for your wind.

Whether you prefer solar to wind or vice versa or simply want your fill of both, rebates, incentives, and tax credits are frequently available to make renewable energy more affordable. To discover what's available, check out the My Watts Estimator at Chooserenewables.com/estimator_start.php. Once you've entered your zip code, the amazing tool will rate your home's solar and wind potential and show you how much you stand to save from federal and state incentives when purchasing a residential system. To delve deeper into specific rebates and incentives, see the database of State Incentives for Renewables & Efficiency, available at dsireusa.org.

Energy Conservation Products

FRIGIDAIRE

Frigidaire.com

For an affordable, energy-efficient refrigerator, check out the Frigidaire FRT18S6AW (about $550), a top-freezer refrigerator that's a great choice for smaller apartments thanks to a slim profile that offers 18 cubic feet of storage space. While the fridge comes with few bells and whistles, it gets the job done with plenty of room for veggies, beer, and leftovers.

HONEYWELL

Yourhome.honeywell.com

The versatile Honeywell FocusPro 6000 series ($70) is an Energy Star–rated digital thermostat that's equipped with an easy-to-read display and is compatible with central air conditioning units as well as electric, gas, or oil furnaces and heat pumps.

LUX

Luxproducts.com

Lux digital thermostats are the affordable, Energy Star–rated choice. *Consumer Reports* touts them for their ease of programming, temperature accuracy, and clear display. They start at around $35 and are available at numerous retailers including Ace Hardware.

PHILLIPS

Consumer.philips.com

The Phillips 42-inch Eco LCD HDTV (model# 42PFL5603D) is the only flat-panel HDTV with a screen size of 27 inches or greater that delivers an excellent picture while using less than 100 watts of energy—91.23 to be exact, less than a 100-watt incandescent lightbulb. When resting in standby mode, the TV sips a miserly .73 watts. At about $1,200, it's priced competitively with other high-quality LCD models.

SMART STRIP POWER STRIP

Smarthomeusa.com

The Smart Strip Power Strip (around $40) comes with 10 outlets; one blue, six white, and three red. When you plug your television into the main outlet (the blue one), all devices plugged into the white outlets become connected to its on/off status. So when you turn your TV on, all the other devices automatically turn on. When you turn your TV, off all the other devices automatically shut off. The three red outlets enable you to operate devices—like lava lamps and curling irons—independently of the TV's on/off status.

SOLATUBE

Solatube.com

To flood your home's interior with natural light all day long, turn to tubular skylights from Solatube. Sunlight is channeled from your rooftop through a narrow tube (that runs through your walls and floorboards) down into your living space. A 10-inch tube and ceiling fixture costs about $300 and is perfect for lighting smaller spaces like bathrooms, laundry rooms, and hallways. The 14-inch model costs about $425 and is great for larger areas like kitchens or living rooms.

WATT STOPPER

Wattstopper.com

A company with a mission to stop energy waste, Watt Stopper sells occupancy motion sensors (under $40) that automatically turn lights on when rooms are occupied and off when rooms are empty. The company's Isolé IDP-3050 8-outlet power strip ($90) applies the same technology to your home's electronics. The power strip's internal occupancy sensor turns on items like computers and other electronics when a room is occupied and off again when it's vacated.

WHIRLPOOL

Whirlpool.com

For a high-quality and energy-efficient, yet budget-conscious, refrigerator, check out the Whirlpool ET1FHTXM (about $850). It offers 21 cubic feet of storage room and includes nice perks like an interior icemaker, water dispenser, spill-control glass shelves, and gallon storage on the door.

Solar and Wind Energy Systems

ANDALAY

Andalay.net

Akeena Solar has developed a sleek, easy-to-install solar panel system called Andalay and has partnered with a solar financing company called Sun Run to help consumers go solar without incurring much of the up front costs. Sun Run enables residents to enter into a long-term contract called a Power Purchase Agreement (PPA), which helps a homeowner purchase the energy being produced by the solar panels on the roof without actually purchasing or leasing the panels.

APPALACHIAN ENERGY

Appalachianenergy.com

Asheville, North Carolina-based Appalachian Energy offers a residential solar energy system that uses solar thermal panels to capture the sun's heat and then uses it to help meet your home's hot water and space heating needs. By doing double-duty on your water and your heat, the system can save between $800 and $1,000 per year on your energy bill for an initial investment of around $5,600 in North Carolina, where state incentives are high.

GROSOLAR

Grosolar.com

Operating throughout the Northeast, Northwest, and Canada, GroSolar is steadily becoming one of the largest solar installers in North America. Where rebates and incentives are available in your state, GroSolar files all of the paperwork on your behalf. And since rebate checks can take a while to arrive, GroSolar charges you the "after rebate" price when installing your system and then collects the incentive checks directly, helping to lower your out-of-pocket costs.

PACWIND

Pacwind.net

PacWind's vertical-access wind turbines (VAWTs) combine some of the most advanced technology in the field with quiet, clean designs that blend into both urban and suburban surroundings. Models of varying size, cost, and wind-generating capacity are available to meet your needs. The entry-level wind generator is the Seahawk. Retail prices start at around $3,000 for the base unit and run to $7,000 for installation, before rebates and incentives.

READY SOLAR

Readysolar.com

ReadySolar offers a deceptively simple modular system, aptly named Solar in a Box, that can be installed quickly and at a reduced cost. Because Solar in a Box is a modular system, you can choose as little or as much solar power as you'd like and then add more capacity over time.

SOLAR CITY

Solarcity.com

In 2008, SolarCity introduced SolarLease, a program that enables homeowners to lease solar panel systems for a low monthly rate and zero money down. SolarCity even provides free repair service and free monitoring for optimal output as part of the performance guarantee that lasts as long as the lease. Leases run for 15 years, after which time you can apply your accumulated monthly payments toward purchasing your system or opt to return it back to the company.

SKYSTREAM 3.7

Skystreamenergy.com

The Skystream 3.7 from Southwest Wind Energy is a sleek, stylized, scaled-down version of the massive wind turbines now used in wind farms. Its "plug and play" capability enables quick installation to begin converting wind into electricity for your home. Depending upon wind speeds, the Skystream can generate anywhere from 40 to 100 percent of a home's electricity needs and typically costs between $6,000 and $8,000 after installation, incentives, and rebates.

Retailers

ECOHAUS

Environmentalhomecenter.com

A growing chain of green home supply stores throughout the northwest United States, Ecohaus offers plenty of products to move your home in a greener direction. Internet shoppers can take advantage of the company's 99-cent deal on Durabright 75-watt equivalent compact fluorescent lightbulbs.

HOME DEPOT

Homedepot.com / ecooptions

Home Depot's Eco Options program makes more than 2,000 green-labeled products available to consumers. Find deals on top-rated n:vision "soft white" or "bright white" compact fluorescent lightbulbs. A 2-pack of 75-watt or 100-watt equivalent bulbs retails for $6.88.

WAL-MART

Walmart.com

Wal-Mart is making shopping for green energy products increasingly afford-able. Purchase a 6-pack of 75 or 100 watt equivalent GE compact fluorescent lightbulbs for $19.32, or $3.22 per bulb.

Information/Education

CHOOSE RENEWABLES

Chooserenewables.com/estimator_start.php.

Find out about rebates, incentives, and tax credits for solar and wind energy in your area by using the My Watts Estimator at Choose Renewables, a retailer of energy-efficient and alternative-energy products. Enter your zip code to learn about your home's solar and wind potential, and see how much you can save from federal and state incentives when purchasing a residential system.

CLEAN POWER FINANCE

Cleanpowerfinance.com

Clean Power Finance is developing relationships with banks across the United States and striking relationships with solar installers to facilitate access to low-rate loans for solar panel systems. If you're in the market for a residential solar system, Clean Power Finance may make an expensive system more financially attractive.

DSIRE (DATABASE OF STATE INCENTIVES FOR RENEWABLES & EFFICIENCY)

Dsireusa.org

Use DSIRE's database to learn about specific renewable energy and energy-efficiency rebates and incentives and favorable financing available to homeowners in your area. The federal government and many state and local governments offer programs that can lower your costs—sometimes by more than 50 percent—for installing a new solar or wind energy system on your home.

ENERGY STAR

Energystar.gov

This jointly administered program of the U.S. Department of Energy and the EPA makes purchasing energy-efficient electronics as easy as choosing products that carry the Energy Star label. Energy Star–rated products are up to 60 percent more energy efficient than standard products and available in more than 50 categories, including digital thermostats, televisions, refrigerators, dishwashers, computers, and other appliances and electronics. The site also maintains a database of home energy auditors who can evaluate your home's energy efficiency and offer recommendations.

EPEAT

Epeat.net

EPEAT (Electronic Product Environmental Assessment Tool) is a program from the Green Electronics Council. Search the site's database to find out which desktop and laptop computers and monitors are the most eco-responsible. Products are evaluated based on lengthy criteria, including energy efficiency, toxicity of materials, recycled and renewable material content, ease of recyclability, product life expectancy, and overall eco-responsibility of the manufacturer.

GREENER CHOICES

Greenerchoices.org

A website run by Consumers Union, the nonprofit publisher of *Consumer Reports*, GreenerChoices.org helps you quickly identify the best-performing green products across numerous categories. The website provides credible, practical, and in-depth information based on its own product reviews. Use it to research the items like energy-efficient refrigerators, air conditioners, dishwashers, and washer/dryers.

GREENYOUR.COM

Greenyour.com is one of the most comprehensive resources for learning how to green just about everything in your life. Type your subject into the "Green Your" search box to get background information, relevant environmental statistics, tips, and product recommendations. Entering "home's energy" into the search box reveals numerous tips and advice on how to begin conserving energy around the house.

THE LAZY ENVIRONMENTALIST

Lazyenvironmentalist.com/energy

I've created a special page to keep Lazy Environmentalist readers updated about ongoing developments in energy efficient products and renewable energy solutions. Tap into green power without tapping too deeply into your checking account.

MYENERGYSTAR.COM

Residents living in the northeast United States can visit Myenergystar.com to scan a database of instant coupons and rebates provided by local power utilities. Deals may include receiving $2 off CFLs that cost more than $2.50 or receiving $30 to $40 off the purchase of a new room air conditioner.

RESNET (RESIDENTIAL ENERGY SERVICES NETWORK)

Natresnet.org

RESNET is a national organization that certifies energy auditors. Visit the site to find a local auditor who will rank your home on a scale of 1 to 100 (one is the most efficient) and generate a list of recommended measures. The ratings can also help you qualify for energy-efficient mortgages, federal tax credits, and become registered as an Energy Star-certified home.

5

Simple Ideas
to
Save Water

Eco-H2O

Fresh drinking water makes up just 1 percent of the earth—a tiny number when you consider that the Environmental Protection Agency (EPA) estimates that the average American household of four uses about 146,000 gallons of water annually or the equivalent of 100 gallons per day per person. And a recent government study cited by the EPA reveals that at least 36 states anticipate water shortages on a local, regional, or statewide level by 2013. Any way you pour it, water is a big deal, but there's good news for Lazy Environmentalists. A few simple and affordable changes can dramatically reduce consumption levels. You can also save money as you save water. The EPA estimates that simple conservation techniques can help the average household reduce its yearly water and sewer bills by $170.

START WITH THE SHOWER

Your daily eight-minute shower uses about 20 gallons of water. Take a shower once a day and it adds up to 7,300 gallons per year. With that much water, a typical family of four could fill its own medium-sized swimming pool, wash 4,152 loads of laundry, or make 166,115 pots of Campbell's soup. Thankfully, you don't have to sacrifice your hygiene to conserve water in the shower. A strategic showerhead is all it takes. WaterPik—creator of the original massage showerhead—recently introduced the Ecoflow. The low-flow showerhead utilizes the company's patented optiFLOW technology to deliver a spray that's comparable to most standard showerheads, yet uses 40 percent less water. Ecoflow uses 1.5 gallons per minute while the standard showerhead gushes out a whopping 2.5 gallons per minute. The showerhead also features a water pause switch so you can prevent waste when waiting for the hot water to kick in or while lathering up. Waterpik-store.com offers fixed-mount Ecoflow models for as low as $14.99 with an instant $5 rebate, and a handheld version is available on the site for $44.99.

Evolve has designed a series of water-saving showerheads that run cold water until the temperature reaches 95 degrees and then stops the flow to a trickle. This way hot water doesn't release until you actually step into the shower and turn the valve to release the flow. With Evolve you can shave, make the bed, bake cupcakes, and catch the end of *Oprah* without wasting gallons of water and all the energy required to heat it. Multiple showerhead styles are available, including the Roadrunner low-flow showerhead, delivering strong water pressure with just 1.59 gallons per minute ($39.95 through Evolveshowerheads.com). The company estimates that the Roadrunner saves eight gallons of water for every five-minute shower when compared to standard showerhead models.

TRADE IN YOUR TOILET

Sit down on some great water savings by opting for a high-efficiency toilet (HET). According to the EPA, toilet flushing accounts for about 30 percent of all indoor residential water use, requiring more water than any other activity in our homes. But the right toilet can change those statistics for the better. In response to rising water demand and looming water shortages, the EPA developed WaterSense, a program that makes it easy for consumers to quickly identify water-efficient products. Toilets that carry the WaterSense label are third-party certified to be at least 20 percent more efficient than today's standard toilets, which reduce flow per flush from an average 1.6 gallons to 1.28 (but toilets installed in your home before 1994 still use 3.5 gallons or more per flush). Visit the program's website at Epa.gov/watersense to find qualifying products plus a list of participating retailers like Vidavici.com, offering one of the widest selections of WaterSense–rated toilets available on the Internet.

Save money on your next toilet purchase by taking advantage of rebates for water-efficient toilets that are sponsored by local city governments throughout North America. For example, residents of Albuquerque, New Mexico, can receive a $125 rebate when replacing a standard toilet model with a water-efficient model. In Sioux Falls, South Dakota, residents are eligible for a $75 rebate when making the switch. Visit Toiletrebate.com to see what incentives may be available to you.

But why send perfectly clean drinking water down the toilet? An AQUS System reuses the water from your bathroom sink for all of your flushing needs. Developed by Water Saver Technologies, the AQUS is a small, simple system that uses a 5 1/2–gallon container inside your sink's vanity (or behind the wall or underneath the floorboards) to capture and filter water as it comes down the sink's drain. The water is run from the container to your toilet's tank with a small tube. Install the AQUS, and you'll be a hero of the planet though you'll barely notice that the device is there. Two people sharing an AQUS-equipped bathroom are estimated to save about 14 gallons of water per day, or 5,000 gallons over the course of a year. The system is available for $295 plus installation. Depending upon your local water and sewage rates, Water Saver Technologies estimates that it usually pays for itself within four to five years. You can find a distributor at Watersavertech.com.

What about the used water (also known as gray water) from your kitchen sink, shower, and dishwasher? While a bigger financial commitment than an AQUS, a whole-house grey water system single-handedly reduces a home's indoor water usage by 30 percent by redirecting used water to all toilets. By law, a household grey water system can only collect used water inside the home to flush toilets; other uses are deemed unsanitary. Canada-based Brac Systems offers a residential system called the Brac 250L ($2,190 at Aquaprosolutions.com), which is optimal for homes with up to six people. Depending on your location, a Brac system could be a wise investment. While the EPA estimates that the average U.S. household pays $523 per year in water and sewage bills, those costs spike in cities like Atlanta, Seattle, and San Diego to well over $1,000 per year. In such cases, a Brac system starts to make both financial and environmental sense.

Reza Pourzia is founder and chief technology officer of Cyber-Rain, a company that has developed a smart sprinkler control system to help homeowners save time, money, and natural resources.

How did you get the idea for Cyber-Rain?

I saw so much wasted water streaming down the street in my neighborhood after people had run their sprinkler systems, and I thought that something had to be done about it. My neighbors and I also hated changing the schedule on our old sprinkler systems. It was hard to figure out how the knobs and dials worked, and it seemed easier to just let it run its schedule than to figure out the cryptic user interface. I knew that a better way would be to have my personal computer set the watering schedule and control the sprinklers. But this idea was not practical until the introduction of new advances in wireless technology. In 2005, I went to a wireless conference where the new IEEE 802.15.4 wireless standard was introduced. I was so impressed at the power and potential of this technology that I decided to quit my consulting job and develop Cyber-Rain.

What is Cyber-Rain's positive environmental impact?

Many people are aware of environmental concerns such as global warming. Fewer are aware of the seriousness of global fresh water shortages and the fact that while population growth is rapidly increasing, the sources of fresh water have remained the same for the last 100 years. Fresh water access is a big risk in many parts of the world, and Cyber-Rain helps tackle these issues by easily and effectively saving thousands of gallons of water by replacing the common "dumb" sprinkler timer. Cyber-Rain also eliminates water run-off, which helps to prevent pesticides, fertilizers, and other chemicals from polluting our rivers and bays.

Are you intentionally targeting dry counties?
We are not intentionally targeting specific areas, although we are surprised at some of the places where demand for Cyber-Rain is particularly strong. For instance, we are selling more units in Texas than in Florida or Arizona. We have also had many requests from other countries, such as Australia, where there has been a severe water shortage. As a small company we are working hard to keep up with the demand in the United States and plan to expand internationally in the near future.

DON'T FORGET THE FAUCET

Next stop on the water conservation journey is the faucet. The EPA estimates that 15 percent of the average household's indoor water use goes toward running kitchen and bathroom faucets. Standard faucets flow at two gallons per minute. WaterSense certified faucets reduce that number to 1.5 gallons per minute—savings that add up over time. Find brands that qualify—including Delta and Moen—at Epa.gov/watersense.

Like your faucets just the way they are? Install faucet aerators instead (you can find them at your local hardware store). Aerators from companies such as Creative Energy Technologies sell for under $7 and reduce faucet flow to 1.5 gallons per minute while still delivering a strong, powerful spray. The company also offers a model that reduces flow to .5 gallons per minute, which may be preferable for bathroom sinks, where a strong flow isn't as important. To date, Neoperl is the only aerator brand approved by WaterSense, but you can expect more to qualify as the WaterSense program gains broader recognition.

UPGRADE YOUR DISHWASHER

Your dishwasher may seem like a guilty necessity, but now there's another reason—besides easy dinner-party cleanup—to love the appliance. A Europe-wide study conducted by scientists at the University of Bonn found that using the latest models of dishwashers saves both energy and water, not to mention time, when compared with washing dishes by hand. This is one area where it's actually preferable to take the lazy route. Though high-quality dishwashers can be as much as $1,000 when you add in perks like adjustable upper racks, hidden controls, sensors, and self-cleaning filters, budget-minded environmentalists can still get the grease off their plates with more economical models. A quick visit to EnergyStar.gov will give you an expansive list of dishwasher models that qualify for the Energy Star label. Dishwashers that are Energy Star rated are at least 41 percent more efficient than standard models. Greenerchoices.org is another solid resource for identifying specific models that clean well while utilizing less energy and water.

The most affordable dishwasher for Lazy Environmentalists is the Whirlpool DU1055XTS(Q) available from Best Buy ($350) and numerous stores across the country. The washer is 43 percent more energy efficient than standard dishwashers and uses just 6 gallons of water per load (remember, the less water you use, the less energy you'll burn to heat it). The DU1055XTS(Q) features five wash cycles, a delay start, adjustable tines, a sani-rinse option, and a self-cleaning filter. The one downside to all this eco-affordability is noise. This particular Whirlpool models lack the sound insulation available in more premium priced models. If you're comfortable springing for a bit more, the Bosch SHE33M02UC (about $550 at online retailers like Homeverything.com) is 80 percent more energy efficient than standard dishwashers, utilizes just 5 gallons of water per load, and is considerably quieter than the Whirlpool DU1055XTS(Q). The Bosch also features a stainless steel tub, adjustable tines, and an adjustable upper rack. And like all Bosch dishwashers, this model uses heat from the wash cycle to dry dishes—yet another way to save energy.

Quality dishwashers are out there, but if the environment and budget are your top concerns, buying a new one should be at the end of your to-do list. According to figures from the U.S. Energy Information Agency, dishwashers are responsible for about 2.5

percent of the average household's energy use. Choosing an Energy Star, water-efficient dishwasher will reduce that energy while saving about 1,000 gallons of water per year. Good news, for sure, but, as outlined above, shifting to low-flow showerheads and high-efficiency toilets makes better economic and environmental sense. For a fraction of the cost of a new dishwasher, these simple eco-upgrades will conserve thousands of gallons of water per year and help you save big on water and sewage bills too.

REDEFINE YOUR WASHING MACHINE

Laundry machines are a different story. According to the EPA, the average household uses about 40 gallons of water per day doing laundry. Energy Star rated washing machines can help you cut that amount by more than half while still getting the grass stains out of your kids' sports uniforms. Ninety percent of the energy expended by clothes washers is used for heating the water, so moving toward an Energy Star, water-efficient model protects the environment and your bank account. As a rule of thumb, front-loading washers are more energy- and water-efficient than top-loaders. They also require less detergent and have shorter drying times (thanks to better moisture extraction during the spin cycle). Front loaders also tend to hover in the upper price stratosphere with top-of-the-line models reaching close to $2,000. A highly rated yet more affordable front-loader is the Frigidaire GLTF2940FS, available from Sears, PC Richards, Amazon.com, and other retailers for as low as $619. The model gets the job done efficiently and can be stacked easily with a dryer. As for top-loaders, the eco-budget winner is the GE WSE5240GWW available from Sears, Home Depot, and other retailers starting at under $400. This GE model offers an ample 3.2 cubic feet of capacity and features an automatic load balancing system that enables the washer to remove more moisture from clothing by spinning at faster speeds (a feature usually reserved for front loaders). As a result, clothes are less damp when they go in the dryer, so they won't have to stay in as long—which will earn you yet another energy saving point.

FIND A NEW WAY TO WATER

There is no thirstier task than landscape irrigation, clocking in at about 30 percent of all household water use. To make matters worse, more than 50 percent of the water we use is wasted as a result of evaporation, wind, improper irrigation system design, or overwatering. Throughout the South and Southwest, water restrictions are already in place in many communities, but installing a smarter irrigation system is another way to keep your lawn and plants thriving while conserving water and cash. The Cyber-Rain XCI is a residential sprinkler control system that allows you to program and control your water output directly from your computer via a wireless link (included with the system). The Cyber-Rain automatically connects to weather satellites to adjust the sprinkler schedule to rain and other climate patterns in your area and lets you view how much water you're saving in real-time on your computer. The system is equipped with wireless controllers for up to eight separate zones (more zones can be added by purchasing additional controllers) and retails for $349.

Flowerbeds and plants will benefit from a drip irrigation system that sends a slow trickle of water directly to your plants' roots from a perforated tube installed beneath the soil's surface. Drip irrigation systems eliminate evaporation waste and off-target sprinkling due to gusts of wind. The systems are affordable (typically as low as $40), though you may want to hire a professional to make sure it's installed properly. The EPA's WaterSense website (Epa. gov/watersense) maintains an active list of landscaping professionals throughout the country who are qualified to install and provide maintenance on such systems. Check out Dripdepot.com to view a wide selection of drip irrigation systems, and be sure to check out the company's simple online tutorials and videos that guide you through the installation process should you choose to DIY. A drip system can also be connected to rain barrels, which collect water from your roof's gutters and downspouts. Try TerraCycle's rain barrels ($99), made by repurposing empty Kendall-Jackson wine barrels. Find them at Sam's Club and major gardening centers around the country.

Water Conservation Products

BOSCH

Boschappliances.com

This leading home-appliances brand offers an affordable entry point for consumers seeking a water- and energy-efficient dishwasher. The Bosch SHE33M02UC ($529 at Amazon.com) is 80 percent more energy efficient than standard dishwashers and utilizes just 5 gallons of water per load. It also features a stainless steel tub, adjustable tines, and an adjustable upper rack.

BRAC SYSTEMS

Bracsystemsbc.com

Brac's household grey water recycling systems single-handedly reduce the average home's water usage by 30 percent by redirecting wastewater generated from showering, bathing, running the dishwasher and kitchen sink, and doing laundry to all toilets for flushing. The Brac 250L ($2190 at Aquaprosolutions.com) is the optimal model for large families with up to six people.

CYBER-RAIN

Cyber-rain.com

The Cyber-Rain XCI ($349) is a residential sprinkler control system that allows you to program and control your water output directly from your computer via a wireless link (included with the system). It automatically connects to weather satellites to adjust the sprinkler schedule to rain and other climate patterns in your area and lets you see how much water you're saving in real-time on your computer.

EVOLVE SHOWERHEADS

Evolveshowerheads.com

Evolve has designed a series of water-saving showerheads that let the cold water run until the water temperature reaches 95 degrees and then stops water flow to a trickle. This way hot water doesn't release until you actually step in the shower and turn the showerhead's valve to release the flow. Multiple showerhead styles are available, including the Roadrunner low-flow showerhead ($39.95), delivering strong water pressure with just 1.59 gallons per minute.

FRIGIDAIRE

Frigidaire

Washing machines can be an expensive proposition, but Frigidaire is making it easier for budget-conscious Lazy Environmentalists to conserve resources while getting the whole wash clean. Check out the front-loading Frigidaire GLTF2940FS, available from Sears, PC Richards, Amazon.com, and other retailers for as low as $619.

GE

Geappliances.com

GE's affordable and resource-efficient top-loading washing machine is the GE WSE5240GWW available at Sears, Home Depot, and other retailers starting at under $400. It offers an ample 3.2 cubic feet of capacity and features an automatic load-balancing system that enables the washer to remove more moisture from clothing by spinning at faster speeds, a feature that helps conserve additional energy by reducing the amount of time clothes spend in the dryer.

HANSGROHE

Hansgrohe-usa.com

Hansgrohe's low-flow showerheads are equipped with the company's EcoAIR technology to reduce water use by 36 percent while delivering strong water pressure. Find them at Faucetdirect.com for as low as $21.70. Talk about an eco-enlightened company: Hansgrohe uses solar power to run its production facility in Offenburg, Germany. Other water-efficient products include faucets and faucet aerators.

NEOPERL

Neoperl.com

Neoperl has been a supplier to the North American faucet industry since its founding in 1928 and currently is the only faucet aerator brand approved by WaterSense. Find its faucet aerators at retailers like Freshwatersystems. com.

TERRACYCLE

Terracycle.net

TerraCycle has applied its expertise in repurposing and recycling to introduce its rain barrels, which transform used Kendall-Jackson oak wine barrels into a solution for collecting water from your roof's downspouts. Purchase the rain barrels for $99 at Sam's Club and major gardening centers around the United States.

SIMPLE IDEAS TO SAVE WATER

WATERPIK

Waterpik.com

Waterpik's Ecoflow low-flow showerheads utilize the company's patented optiFLOW technology to deliver a spray that's comparable to most standard showerheads, yet uses 40 percent less water (just 1.5 gallons per minute). The showerhead also features a water pause switch so you can prevent waste when waiting for the hot water to kick in or while lathering up. Purchase the fixed mount Ecoflow ($14.99) or a handheld version ($44.99) at Waterpik-store.com.

WATER SAVER TECHNOLOGIES

Watersavertech.com

The AQUS System from Water Saver Technologies reuses the water from your bathroom sink for all of your flushing needs. The AQUS uses a 5 1/2-gallon container inside your sink's vanity to capture and filter water as it comes down the sink's drain. The water is run from the container to your toilet's tank with a small tube. The simple system can save an average couple about 5,000 gallons of water per year and is available for $295 plus installation.

WHIRLPOOL

Whirlpool.com

One of the most resource-efficient and affordable dishwashers, the Whirlpool DU1055XTS(Q) is available from Best Buy for $350. It is 43 percent more energy efficient than standard dishwashers and uses just 6 gallons of water per load; it also features five wash cycles, a delay start, adjustable tines, a sani-rinse option, and a self-cleaning filter.

Retailers

AQUAPRO SOLUTIONS

Aquaprosolutions.com

A one-stop shop for your water conservation and filtration needs, Aquapro Solutions offers high-efficiency toilets, low-flow showerheads, faucet aerators, and grey water systems from Water Saver Technologies and Brac Systems.

CLEAN AIR GARDENING

Cleanairgardening.com

Start your search here for affordable rain barrels, electric-powered lawn mowers, and everything else you need to create a water- and energy-efficient garden. You can also purchase affordable natural organic lawn and gardening supplies.

CREATIVE ENERGY TECHNOLOGIES
Cetsolar.com
This retailer offers a wide selection of products designed to help you easily conserve water and energy. From solar cell phone chargers and pool heaters to low-flow showerheads and faucet aerators, Creative Energy Technologies has got you covered.

DRIP DEPOT
Dripdepot.com
Visit Dripdepot.com to view a wide selection of drip irrigation systems, ranging in price from about $15 to $80. If you plan to install your own system, take advantage of the company's simple online tutorials and videos that can guide easily you through the process.

VIDAVICI
Vidavici.com
Vidavici offers an extensive line of WaterSense-labeled water-efficient toilets and faucets. You can also shop for other water-efficient products by room or brand. Check out the "Buying Guides" section to get tips on selecting the right products to match your home's needs.

Information/Education

CONSUMER SEARCH
Consumersearch.com
This website reviews the product reviews from other sources to determine which are the most credible and therefore which products are truly the top-rated choices for consumers. Read its reports about products like dishwashers and washer/drying machines to learn which products are truly the most water- and energy-efficient.

GREENYOUR.COM
Greenyour.com is one of the most comprehensive resources for learning how to green just about everything in your life. Type your subject into the "Green Your" search box to get background information, relevant environmental statistics, tips, and product recommendations. Entering "home's water" into the search box reveals numerous tips and advice on how to begin conserving water around the house.

GREENER CHOICES

Greenerchoices.org

A website run by Consumers Union, the nonprofit publisher of *Consumer Reports*, GreenerChoices.org helps you quickly identify the best-performing green products across numerous categories. The website provides credible, practical, and in-depth information based on its own product reviews. Use it to find water- and energy-efficient dishwashers and clothes washers. Other major appliances, like refrigerators and air conditioners, are also reviewed.

THE LAZY ENVIRONMENTALIST

Lazyenvironmentalist.com/water

I've created a special page to keep Lazy Environmentalist readers updated about ongoing developments in water-efficient products. Get cutting-edge strategies for easily conserving water without compromising the way you live.

TERRY LOVE

Terrylove.com/crtoilet.htm

Terry Love, owner of Love Plumbing and Remodel, has done the world a tremendous service by having personally installed and tested many high-efficiency toilets (HETs) in his own home. Read his reviews to get the inside scoop on how these toilets really perform and determine which model is right for you.

TOILET REBATE

Toiletrebate.com

Just as the name implies, Toilet Rebate uses Google Maps technology to help consumers pinpoint cities throughout North America that offer rebates on water-efficient toilets. Rebates can range up to $200 for a new model. Check the site to see what rebates may be available to you.

WATERSENSE

Epa.gov/watersense

WaterSense is a program sponsored by the EPA and patterned after the Energy Star program to help homeowners find water-efficient products that conserve water and save money. Products such as toilets that carry the WaterSense label are third-party certified to be at least 20 percent more efficient than today's standard toilets. Visit the program's website to find qualifying products plus a list of participating retailers.

6

Righteous Real Estate +Green Remodeling

There's no quicker shortcut to a modern green lifestyle than moving into an eco-friendly home situated within an eco-minded community. When it comes to living green—really living green—it starts with earth-friendly heating and cooling systems and healthful building materials that have been used to create a properly insulated home that requires minimal amounts of energy. Your eco-impact will also be dramatically reduced if that home was also equipped with energy-efficient lighting and appliances and water-efficient plumbing fixtures. And if you opt for a neighborhood with sidewalk-lined streets that are ideal for quick strolls to the local grocery store, café, park, playground, or school—not to mention the local train, subway, or bus stop—then you'll really have gone a long way toward elevating your eco-status. Some call this living green. Others call it getting a life. However you choose to define it, in many parts of the country you don't have to pay top dollar for the privilege.

That's because thousands of real estate developers and home builders across the United States are embracing environmentally smart building practices. They're building high-performance homes that qualify for discounted mortgage rates (making them easier to afford) and rise in market value faster than conventional homes (making them smarter to own). Both national and local green home certifications make it easy to identify green properties, and the addition of green home features in the Multiple Listing Service (databases that help real estate brokers find information on properties for sale) in certain parts of the country make them increasingly easy to locate.

One of the easiest places to live like a Lazy Environmentalist is in the Pacific Northwest, where green homes in places like King

County, Washington—encompassing Seattle and its suburbs—already account for more than 16 percent of all new home sales. Prominent residential redevelopment projects like the High Point in Western Seattle prove that green living is nothing more than really good living. That is, of course, if good living means homes built with front porches that foster a feeling of neighborliness and walkable neighborhoods that provide quick access to open outdoor spaces, trails, playgrounds, and a host of other amenities. All homes at High Point are constructed to the green standards of Built Green, a local environmentally friendly building program serving King and Snohomish Counties in Washington State, and include features to promote energy and water conservation and healthier indoor air quality.

In fact, the entire High Point development has been created with an eye toward reducing the overall impact of everyone who lives there. Sidewalks are built with porous cement to avoid storm-water runoff and to allow water to replenish groundwater tables; outdoor areas are landscaped with drought-tolerant plants to support water conservation; residents can quickly zip into downtown Seattle using public transportation (leaving the car and its pollutants at home); and a public community-wide recycling center is on-site to make chucking the recyclables in the appropriate bin a cinch.

More than 200 homes have already been completed and sold with housing styles ranging from contemporary townhomes to carriage houses to single-family detached homes. By the time the project is finished, more than 1,600 residential units will have been built on the 120-acre site. And because High Point is a mixed-income community offering subsidized low-income, affordable, and market rate housing, people of all socioeconomic backgrounds get to participate in this new paradigm of environmental activism, which showcases how living green not only improves the health of the planet but also improves the quality of our lives.

Built Green isn't the only certification to ensure that homes are eco-conscious. Houses in and around Seattle and other nearby communities are also qualifying for national environmental certifications such as Energy Star—for homes that are at least 20 to 30 percent more energy efficient than standard homes—and LEED for Homes (Leadership in Environmental and Energy Design), a green building rating system set by the U.S. Green Building Council that rates homes on a broad of range of criteria like selection of building materials, energy and water efficiency, renewable energy, and recycling of construction site waste. But how much do these houses cost? Well, with increasing availability comes greater affordability. A groundbreaking 2008 market report issued by Seattle-based GreenWorks Realty, one of the leading green real estate brokerages in the country, found that environmentally certified (including Built Green, Energy Star, and LEED) houses in King County have a median price of $487,000, just 4 percent more than the $470,000 median price for standard homes. And though these homes are on average 25 percent smaller than standard homes—smaller houses require fewer materials to build and less energy to operate —those built to green standards sold 18 percent faster than their conventional counterparts. Size does seem to matter, but not as much as saving money on energy bills and doing our part for the planet.

Lazy Environmentalists who prefer fast-paced urban living are not without affordable eco-options. Green condos and apartments are popping up in cities across the country, and in many cases their presence is helping to revitalize inner city communities. Take 1400 on 5th in the Harlem neighborhood of New York City. Developed by Full Spectrum, a leader in developing mixed-income green residential properties in emerging urban markets, the 128-unit condo building relies on a geothermal heating and cooling system, a renewable energy source that draws upon water deep beneath the building, to help reduce energy costs for residents by 70 percent. The building itself is comprised of materials that contain 60 percent recycled content; low-VOC wall coverings and carpets support healthy indoor air quality; and every single unit has floors made of bamboo, a rapidly renewable resource and a wonderful alternative to wood. Energy Star appliances and low-flow water conservation fixtures are also standard. Choose from one-, two-, and three-bedroom simplex and duplex condos or three- and four-bedroom triplex units. Only a portion are sold at market rate prices, while the bulk of the units are subsidized and available only to families with incomes ranging between $52,000 and $103,700. Full Spectrum's visionary co-founder Carlton Brown is demonstrating that building green can be a strategy that works for middle-income families, and he's proving it in the heart of New York City, home to some of the most expensive real estate on the planet.

Brown and his team at Full Spectrum are just getting started. The Kalahari is their second green residential building in Harlem, featuring 249 units, 120 of which have been set aside for families with moderate- to middle-incomes levels. Whereas 1400 on 5th relies on a geothermal renewable energy, the Kalahari draws upon renewable solar and wind energy for 25 percent of its energy needs. In Trenton, New Jersey, Full Spectrum is developing the Trenton Town Center, a massive 700,000-square-foot green building project that will house shops, offices, and nearly 200 residential condominium units that will reduce energy use by more than 50 percent compared to standard buildings. Other green projects are under way in Jackson, Mississippi, and New Orleans, Louisiana—green living recognizes no geographic boundaries.

Affordable green residential housing is also booming in North Carolina, thanks to a concerted effort by builders to comply with HealthyBuilt Homes, a voluntary statewide, eco-certification program. Nowhere is the trend more prevalent than in Asheville, North Carolina, a forward-thinking city situated in a majestic valley bordered by the Blue Ridge Mountains to the east and the Great Smoky Mountains to the West. Uber-trendy *Wallpaper* magazine has ranked Asheville "the #1 Urban Haven in the World," and Natural Home magazine ranks West Asheville as the top eco-neighborhood in the country. Equal parts hip and funky and increasingly sophisticated to boot, West Asheville is home to newly built green developments like Hudson Street Cottages, an eight-unit condo community. Priced at $239,000, each 3-bedroom unit features a solar hot water system used for domestic hot water needs (think shower and dishwasher) and for radiant heat, a home heating system created by running hot water through pipes installed beneath the floor boards. Units also include low-flow plumbing

Mark Mathieu is founder and CEO of Walk Score, a company with a mission to promote walkable communities.

How did you get the idea for Walk Score?
We noticed that our urban planner friends used the phrase "walkable neighborhood" as a kind of shorthand for things you want in a great place to live: well-designed, vibrant, healthy, sustainable, culturally rich, and diverse. We'd seen a number of academic studies that measured walkability, but they only measured certain neighborhoods and were difficult to understand (e.g., how does the floor area ratio of a building help me figure out whether a neighborhood is walkable?!). We created Walk Score so that anyone can type in an address, get their Walk Score, and see what's nearby. We hope all real estate listings will eventually have a Walk Score attached: two bedroom, two bath, Walk Score 85.

What is Walk Score's positive environmental impact?
Walk Score helps people find more walkable places to live. Where you choose to live can be one of the most important decisions you make for your health and the health of the planet. You can choose a car-dependent lifestyle that creates more pollution, increases your waistline, and decreases interaction with other people—or you can choose a walkable neighborhood where your feet are marvels of zero pollution transportation. Sure, walking is slower than driving, but that extra 15 minutes it takes to get exercise and chat with your neighbors on the way to do your errands might be the best 15 minutes of your day.

If we all start walking everywhere, who will buy all of this expensive gas?
Don't worry, it will be a while before zero pollution air travel hits the market. People do not have wings, which is an okay excuse to board an airplane, but people do have feet so there are fewer excuses not to walk.

fixtures, bamboo floors, and low-VOC paints. Close by you'll find Gaia, a new green community featuring 15 homes built around a common green plus a communal organic garden and an outdoor meditation space. HealthyBuilt- and Energy Star–certified homes start at $169,000.

In Asheville's River Arts district, home to numerous galleries and working art studios, Mica Lofts transforms a former mica processing factory into modern loft-style condominiums. Talk about a charming way to reduce your eco-impact—Mica's units feature the original wood flooring, brick walls, and exposed hemlock posts and beams, but are updated with countertops made of recycled glass, low-VOC wall paints, and Energy Star lighting. One bedrooms (830 square feet) begin at $226,000. In downtown Asheville you'll find Zona Lofts, a 15-story, 162-unit condo high-rise featuring a rooftop solar hot water system; a rainwater collection and storage system for toilet flushing; Energy Star appliances and lighting, low-flow plumbing fixtures, bamboo floors, and low-VOC paints. The best part for the super-lazy is the three-way recyclable trash chute on every floor that makes separating and discarding your recyclables about as simple as opening your front door. Units start at $122,000 and reach up to $499,000 and can be leased, leased-to-own, or bought.

Washington or North Carolina not in your future? The quickest way to find a qualifying green home in your area is to search the website of your local or regional green building program. The National Association of Homebuilders maintains an online database of such programs. Find it by visiting Nahbgreen.org and clicking on the "Who Is Green" tab. The Energy Star website at Energystar.gov also maintains a database of several thousand builders across the United States who are constructing Energy Star–qualified homes. Greenhomesforsale.com lists available properties across the country with eco-credentials such as geothermal heating or solar power that are offered directly by homeowners and real estate brokers. Moderngreenliving.com lists green residential condos, apartments, and neighborhood housing developments, as does Listedgreen. com. You can also solicit the assistance of a real estate broker to help you in your search. EcoBroker offers a green certification program for real estate brokers and lists the contact information of those who are certified on its website at EcoBroker.com. And banks are making it a bit more affordable to go green. In 2008, Countrywide Home Loans introduced an interest rate reduction of .125 percent on loans to homebuyers for newly built, third-party-verified green homes. The program is currently available in Arkansas, Colorado, Iowa, Idaho, Minnesota, Montana, Nebraska, North Dakota, Oregon, South Dakota, Utah, Washington, and Wyoming. Many banks also offer additional financing for implementing energy-efficient upgrades to your home through Energy Efficiency Mortgages (EEMs). Banks are beginning to recognize that when you make your home energy efficient you lower your monthly energy costs and therefore have more funds available to pay back a larger mortgage.

GIVE YOUR HOME AN ECO-FACELIFT

Moving is not the only way to live green. You can also upgrade your current home with planet-friendly features. Start with the floors and walls, as they're prime candidates for an affordable makeover. Other areas of your home may require a bit more creativity to maximize the green features and minimize the cost. While green designers and entrepreneurs are rapidly developing breakthrough materials and products—like Paperstone, a strong, sleek countertop surface made of up to 100 percent recycled paper, and Icestone, a colorful, durable tile or countertop surface made of recycled glass and concrete—the prices for these stunning choices aren't quite within reach for budget-conscious consumers. But let's quickly put this in perspective: A few short years ago—like as recently as 2004—few, if any, stylish green building products existed! That many of us are currently feeling frustrated by the cost of green building products is a testament to how quickly green design has improved. We may have to wait a couple more years for many green building products to become affordable, but in the meantime, Lazy Environmentalists can still get their hands on high-quality, eco-intelligent products by knowing where to turn.

COLOR YOUR WALLS WITH PLANET-PROTECTING PAINT

Our walls surround us, so it's natural that the way they look would influence our sense of well-being and comfort. This is why it makes sense to use high-quality paints that also eliminate what are known as VOCs (Volatile Organic Compounds), the solvents found in standard paints that contaminate indoor air. That strong, unpleasant odor accompanying a new paint job is not your brother's B.O.—it's VOCs seeping into the air. Unfortunately, they continue to do so as long as the paint remains on the wall. But fortunately, healthier, low- or zero-VOC options are priced competitively with most premium paints. While there's no widely available budget option in this product category, this is one area in which it's advisable to trade up for quality. (Plus, splurging on a few gallons of high-quality paint is still one of the most cost-effective ways to upgrade your home's aesthetic and improve its indoor air quality). Larger companies such as Benjamin Moore, Sherwin Williams, and Olympic offer lines that are low or zero-VOC. Smaller, innovative paint companies like Bioshield, Yolo Colorhouse, and Mythic Paint do too. Professionals who run green building supply companies tend to prefer the indoor and outdoor zero-VOC paints and finishes from AFM Safecoat. The company's Ayurveda Essence collection features 108 colors in three distinct palettes (Vata, Pitta, and Kapha) and is designed to bring beautiful hues as well as the ancient healing properties of Ayurveda into your home. A quart of paint costs about $12 and a gallon costs about $36. AFM Safecoat paints have been awarded Indoor Air Quality Gold Certification by Scientific Certification Systems (a leading third-party testing and certification service) for achieving the most stringent air-quality standards in North America.

Those who live in the Pacific Northwest can take advantage of one the most innovative recycling programs in the country—high-quality, affordable, and 100 percent recycled natural latex paint. Called MetroPaint, the program is administered by Metro, Portland, Oregon's regional governing body. Think about those half-full tins of unused paint sitting in the basement or garage. By collaborating with local hazardous waste facilities, MetroPaint processes unused paint into new paint. Prices are pretty much unbeatable at $6 to $10 for a gallon and $25 to $44 for five gallons. What's fascinating about the process is that when paints of a similar hue are all collected and combined in a 300-gallon sized vat, the resulting mixture always defaults to the same color. This makes it possible for MetroPaint to offer a consistent color palette for its customers who also love the paints for their high quality and easy application.

GREEN YOUR FLOORS

Flooring is a category in which you can really make an eco-difference. Naturally made linoleum is being revitalized for twenty-first century living by Switzerland-based Forbo. The company's Marmoleum Click tiles are easy for anyone to install; they just click together without need for nails or glue. Water resistant, durable, easy to clean and naturally beautiful, Forbo's Marmoleum Click linoleum tiles are made with natural ingredients including linseed oil, pigments, cork flour, limestone, pine rosin, and pine flour from managed European forests. The backing is made of natural jute. Eighteen different colors are available and can be mixed and matched. The price per square foot starts at around $4.

Rapidly renewable materials like bamboo are also versatile and eco-friendly. Smith & Fong, EcoTimber, and Teragren are a few of the highly regarded companies working with this new take on hardwood floors. EcoTimber's strand-woven bamboo flooring receives particularly high marks for its incredible strength and durability. Prices from these companies typically range between and $5 and $7 per square foot. While lower-priced bamboo flooring products are available, the companies mentioned here have developed strong reputations within the green building community for quality, durability, aesthetics, and low-toxicity (these companies minimize the use of dangerous, formaldehyde-based glues during manufacturing).

Budget-friendly cork flooring is yet another way to utilize a natural, rapidly renewable material, and some of the most affordable options available come from Texas-based Amcork. Made from the renewable bark of the cork oak tree and treated with zero-VOC finishes, AmCork's flooring planks and tiles come in numerous colors and patterns and start at $2.50 per square foot. Whereas bamboo is extremely strong and sturdy, cork is naturally durable yet more forgiving and very soft underfoot. As an added perk, cork also functions as a headache-relieving sound barrier for multilevel homes.

Wood floors can get into the budget green act too. The best way to locate affordable reclaimed or sustainably harvested wood flooring is to visit local green building supply stores. They're cropping up all over the country and often carry locally made products that are otherwise tough to locate. For example, Ecohaus stores in Portland, Seattle, and Bellevue, Washington, carry Green River reclaimed hardwood flooring starting at $4.29 per square foot. In Asheville, North Carolina, Build It Naturally works with a local mill to offer stunning reclaimed wood flooring starting at $6 at per square foot.

CONSIDER A COOLER CARPET (OR RUG)

Begin your quest for affordable, eye-popping, earth-friendly rug design with FLOR. A division of Interface, the largest modular carpet tile manufacturer in the world and quite possibly the most eco-enlightened company in the known universe, FLOR puts the power of design in your hands. You select modular tile colors and patterns and mix and match as you please, creating unique wall-to-wall carpeting or area rugs. The company's website, Flor.com, has design tools to help you dream up your own creations. Collections like Fedora are made with 80 percent recycled polyester, feature a palette of bold, modern colors, and retail for $2.60 per square foot. Other collections incorporate natural materials like hemp and wool and newer materials like PLA (a fiber made from corn). All FLOR products have extremely low VOC levels. While many of the tile collections utilize nylon or polyester, both of which are derived from petroleum, FLOR is committed to continuously incorporating as much recycled content as possible into its flooring. The company's R&R (Return & Recycle) program lets you mail old tiles back to the company—free of charge—to be recycled into new carpet tiles. FLOR's eco-initiatives are part of Interface's Mission Zero program, which is steering the company toward zero (or negative) environmental impact by 2020. Since the program began in 1994, the company has reduced landfill waste by 63 percent, energy obtained from fossil fuels by 45 percent, and overall greenhouse gas emissions by 60 percent. To track the company's environmental progress, visit Florisgreen.com.

West Elm wins the award for eco-conscious rugs most likely to be found in your local mall. The rapidly growing retailer offers an affordable series of contemporary area rugs using natural, renewable materials like wool, seagrass, and jute. Clean contemporary patterns feature flowers, circles, and beanstalks. Prices start at $129 for a 5x8-foot rug and go up to $749 for a 9x12-foot rug. Turn to Gaiam.com for all-weather indoor or outdoor rugs made from recycled soda bottles. Handcrafted by Thai artisans, the ultra-durable rugs are available in Oriental, Turkish, or floral patterns and come in several different colors. Prices start at $39 for a 4x6-foot area rug and go up to $89 for a 6x9-foot version.

SALVAGE MATERIALS

Reusing is a core Lazy Environmentalist tenet—as long as it's easy and convenient to do. And when it comes to home renovation, the easiest places to turn for high-quality, affordable, recycled building elements are the retailers that specialize in these salvaged materials. The Building Material Reuse Association maintains an extensive online directory of retailers throughout the United States (see Buildingreuse.org). A quick search reveals providers in every state who offer everything from walnut flooring to granite countertops. Remember, just because a material is reused doesn't mean that it will necessarily look reused. And installing reused materials in your home means that you're respecting your wallet while extending the useful life of quality products (and keeping them out of landfills).

The Green Project, a nonprofit organization based in New Orleans, Louisiana, shifted its salvaging operations into high gear after Hurricane Katrina inflicted unprecedented damage on the city. In many neighborhoods where abandoned houses have been condemned, the Green Project sends in trained deconstruction teams to recover as much reusable building material as possible before the houses are wrecked. As much as 70 percent of buildings are recovered. The high-quality materials are sold back to community members, usually at drastically discounted prices through the company's local warehouse store to aid in the city's reconstruction. Like MetroPaint in Portland, Oregon, The Green Project also recycles and reprocesses leftover paint and makes it available to residents for $5 a gallon.

Other major salvage warehouse retailers like Second Use in Seattle, Washington, divert as much as 60 to 100 tons of quality reusable building materials from the landfill each month. You'll find items such as appliances, cabinets, sinks, countertops, doors, flooring, lighting fixtures, lumber, tiles, plumbing fixtures, windows, and more—all at reasonable prices. Driftwood Salvage, based in East Palo-Alto, California, not only sells salvaged materials, but also uses reused materials to create its own line of reclaimed products at affordable prices. Reclaimed wood butcher block countertops sell for about $20 per square foot. Finely crafted garden trellises are available for $179.99, and a sturdy reclaimed wood compost box sells for $199.99. Habitat for Humanity also maintains a chain of salvaged material retail warehouses throughout the United States and Canada called ReStores. Retailers such as Home Depot often donate surplus materials to ReStores in exchange for tax deductions, as do local contractors with excess materials from job sites. Proceeds from sales support Habitat's mission to build low-income affordable housing. As such, ReStores deliver value to you, the environment, and community members who are most in need—a triple Lazy Environmentalist win.

Residential Developments, Developers, and Realtors

FULL SPECTRUM

Fullspectrumny.com

Full Spectrum is a leader in developing mixed-income green residential properties in emerging urban markets. In the Harlem neighborhood of New York City, the real estate developer has built 1400 on 5th, a 128-unit condo building that uses geothermal renewable energy and energy-efficient strategies to reduce energy costs by 70 percent. Nearby, the Kalahari, a 249-unit building, draws upon solar and wind energy to help meet its power needs. Both buildings set aside a major portion of units for moderate- to middle-income families. A similar affordable green housing strategy is being adopted at Full Spectrum's developments in Trenton, New Jersey, and Jackson, Mississippi.

GREENWORKS REALTY

Greenworksrealty.com

Seattle-based GreenWorks Realty is one of the leading green real estate brokerages in the country and an excellent resource for tapping into the green building boom under way in the Pacific Northwest. In 2008, the firm released a study that found that environmentally certified houses in and around Seattle have a median price of $487,000, just 4 percent more than the $470,000 median price for standard homes, yet the study also found that the green homes sell 18 percent faster.

THE HIGH POINT

Thehighpoint.com

The High Point development in Western Seattle, Washington, is a mixed-income green community. The walkable neighborhoods provide quick access to open outdoor spaces, trails, playgrounds, and a host of other amenities. Homes are built with front porches to foster a feeling of neighborliness and constructed to the green standards of Built Green and include features to promote energy and water conservation and healthier indoor air quality.

HUDSON STREET COTTAGES

Ecoconceptsrealty.com/properties/hudson-cottages

Hudson Street Cottages is an eight-unit condo community located in West Asheville, North Carolina. Priced at $239,000, each 3-bedroom unit features a solar hot water system used for domestic hot water needs (think shower and dishwasher) and for radiant heat (a home heating system created by running hot water through pipes installed beneath the floor boards). Units also include low-flow plumbing fixtures, bamboo floors, and low-VOC paints.

GAIA
Ecoconceptsrealty.com / Gaia.htm
Gaia is a new green community in West Asheville, North Carolina, featuring 15 homes built around a common green plus a communal organic garden and an outdoor meditation space. The Energy Star–certified and HealthyBuilt homes are available for sale starting at $169,000.

MICA LOFTS
Micavillagelofts.com
Mica Lofts is a former mica processing factory in Asheville, North Carolina, that has been transformed into modern loft-style condominiums. To conserve resources, Mica's units feature the original wood flooring, brick walls, and exposed hemlock posts and beams, but are updated with countertops made of recycled glass, low-VOC wall paints, and Energy Star lighting. One bedrooms (830 square feet) begin at $226,000.

ZONA LOFTS
Zonalofts.com
In downtown Asheville, North Carolina, you'll find Zona Lofts, a 15-story, 162-unit condo high-rise featuring a rooftop solar hot water system; a rainwater collection and storage system for toilet flushing; Energy Star appliances and lighting, low-flow plumbing fixtures, bamboo floors, and low-VOC paints. Units start at $122,000 and reach up to $499,000 and can be leased, leased-to-own, or bought.

Home Remodeling Products

AMCORK
Amcork.com
Texas-based Amcork offers cork flooring planks and tiles that are available in numerous colors and patterns and start at just $2.50 per square foot. Cork is naturally durable yet forgiving and very soft underfoot. As an added perk, cork also functions as a headache-relieving sound barrier for multilevel homes.

AFM SAFECOAT
Afmsafecoat.com
Professionals who run green building supply companies tend to prefer the indoor and outdoor zero-VOC paints and finishes from AFM Safecoat. The company's Ayurveda Essence collection features 108 colors in three distinct

palettes (Vata, Pitta, and Kapha) and is designed to bring beautiful hues as well as the ancient healing properties of Ayurveda into your home. A quart of paint costs about $12 and a gallon costs about $36.

ECOTIMBER
Ecotimber.com
EcoTimber's low-VOC bamboo flooring is durable, attractive, and affordable with prices starting at around $5.50 per square foot. You'll also find beautiful reclaimed wood and FSC-certified wood flooring options from this company that's been an industry leader since its founding in 1992.

FLOR
Flor.com
FLOR offers modular rug tiles in a wide assortment of colors and patterns. Collections like Fedora are made with 80 percent recycled polyester and retail for $2.60 per square foot. Other collections incorporate natural materials like hemp and wool and newer materials like PLA (a fiber made from corn). All FLOR products have extremely low VOC levels. The company's R&R (Return & Recycle) program lets you mail old tiles back to the company—free of charge—to be recycled into new carpet tiles.

MARMOLEUM CLICK
Themarmoleumstore.com
For a natural flooring solution that's super-stylish and simple to install, try Marmoleum Click tiles. The linoleum tiles are made with natural ingredients including linseed oil, pigments, cork flour, limestone, pine rosin, and pine flour from managed European forests and include a backing made of natural jute. The tiles click together without nails or glue. Prices start at around $4 per square foot.

METRO PAINT
Metropaint.info
In Portland, Oregon, MetroPaint administers an innovative recycling programs that makes high-quality, natural latex paint extremely affordable. By collaborating with local hazardous waste facilities, MetroPaint processes unused paint and recycles it into new paint. Prices are $6 to $10 for a gallon and $25 to $44 for five gallons.

SMITH & FONG

Plyboo.com

Look for well-priced bamboo flooring marketed under the name Plyboo from Smith & Fong. In 2008, the company became the first ever to receive FSC certification for bamboo products, ensuring that responsible management practices are in place and that no irrigation, pesticides, or fertilizers are used in growing the bamboo.

TERAGREN

Teragren.com

Look to Teragren for hard, durable bamboo flooring at affordable prices. Available in natural colors as well as darker stains to complement many interior decors, Teragren's bamboo flooring retails for around $6 per square foot. The company goes to great lengths to ensure that its workers receive fair wages for their labor and that its products are made of the highest-grade bamboo.

Retailers

BUILD IT NATURALLY

Builditnaturally.com

Based in Asheville, North Carolina, Build It Naturally is a green building supply company specializing in natural, nontoxic, recycled, and renewable building materials. The company also works with a local mill to offer stunning and affordably priced reclaimed wood flooring starting at $6 at per square foot.

ECOHAUS

Environmentalhomecenter.com

A growing chain of green home supply stores throughout the northwest United States, Ecohaus offers plenty of products to move your home in a greener direction. Look for the company's locally sourced Green River reclaimed hardwood flooring starting at $4.29 per square foot.

DRIFTWOOD SALVAGE

Driftwoodsalvage.com

Based in East Palo-Alto, California, Driftwood Salvage not only sells salvaged building materials but also uses reused materials to create its own line of reclaimed products at affordable prices. Reclaimed wood butcher block countertops sell for about $20 per square foot. Finely crafted garden trellises are available for $179.99 and a sturdy reclaimed wood compost box sells for $199.99.

GAIAM

Gaiam.com

For all-weather indoor or outdoor rugs made from recycled soda bottles, visit Gaiam.com. Handcrafted by Thai artisans, the ultradurable rugs are available in Oriental, Turkish, or floral patterns and come in several different colors. Prices start at $39 for a 4x6-foot area rug and go up to $89 for a 6x9-foot version. You'll also find plenty of other affordable and attractive products to choose from at this green living retailer.

GREEN DEPOT

Greendepot.com

With five retail locations in the Northeast (and more on the way), Green Depot is emerging as one of the country's leading green building supply companies. You can shop for many of the latest green building products directly through the company's website, learn more about green building terms, standards, certifications, and concepts in the Green Building 101 section, and correspond directly with green building pioneer and Green Depot's in-house expert Paul Novak to answer your most pressing green questions.

THE GREEN PROJECT

Thegreenproject.org

The Green Project is a nonprofit organization based in New Orleans, Louisiana, that sends trained deconstruction teams to recover as much reusable building material as possible from houses that are being torn down. As much as 70 percent of buildings are recovered. The high-quality materials are sold back to community members usually at drastically discounted prices through the company's local warehouse store to aid in the city's post-Katrina reconstruction.

HABITAT RESTORES

Habitat.org / env / restores.aspx

Habitat ReStores is a chain of salvaged material retail warehouses located throughout the United States and Canada. Proceeds from sales support Habitat for Humanity's mission to build low-income affordable housing. Purchasing items from these stores is a great way to find quality products at a fraction of the retail price while simultaneously giving back to the community and keeping useful items out of landfills.

SECOND USE
Seconduse.com

Second Use is a salvaged building material retailer based in Seattle, Washington, that sells appliances, cabinets, sinks, countertops, doors, flooring, lighting fixtures, lumber, tiles, plumbing fixtures, windows, and more—all at reasonable prices. As a result, Second Use is able to divert as much as 60 to 100 tons of quality reusable building materials from the landfill each month.

WEST ELM
Westelm.com

West Elm offers an affordable series of contemporary area rugs using natural, renewable materials like wool, seagrass, and jute. Clean contemporary patterns feature flowers, circles, and beanstalks. Prices start at $129 for a 5x8-foot rug and go up to $749 for a 9x12-foot rug. You'll also find a wide assortment of reasonably priced organic cotton bedding and bath products.

Information/Education

100KHOUSE.COM

Follow the green building adventure as Post Green, a real estate developer in Philadelphia, Pennsylvania, strives to build a two-bedroom, modern green townhouse on a $100,000 budget. Read past blog entries to see which building materials and strategies are helping to make the project possible.

BUILDING MATERIALS REUSE ASSOCIATION
Buildingreuse.org

The Building Material Reuse Association maintains an extensive online directory of salvaged building material retailers throughout the United States. A quick search reveals providers in every state who offer deals on everything from walnut flooring to granite countertops. Remember, just because it is reused doesn't mean it will necessarily look reused.

COUNTRYWIDE HOME LOANS
Countrywide.com

In 2008, Countrywide Home Loans introduced an interest rate reduction of .125 percent on loans to homebuyers for newly built, third-party-verified green homes. The program is currently available in Arkansas, Colorado, Iowa, Idaho, Minnesota, Montana, Nebraska, North Dakota, Oregon, South Dakota, Utah, Washington, and Wyoming.

ECOBROKER INTERNATIONAL

Ecobroker.com

EcoBroker offers a green certification program for real estate brokers and lists the contact information of those who are certified on its website. More than 3,000 professionals across the United States have obtained the certification.

ENERGY STAR

Energystar.com

Visit the Energy Star website to search a database of several thousand builders across the United States that are currently building Energy Star–qualified homes that lower energy costs by at least 20 to 30 percent compared with standard homes. Energy Star is a jointly administered program of the U.S. Department of Energy and the EPA that helps consumers easily reduce their use of energy. In addition to homes, you'll find Energy Star–rated products in categories like televisions, refrigerators, dishwashers, and computers.

GREEN BUILDING TALK

Greenbuildingtalk.com

Use the discussion forums at Greenbuildingtalk.com to have your green building–related questions can answered by other homeowners who share their experience and by professionals who share their expertise. The site is an excellent resource for finding out information like whether a contractor is overcharging you or where to locate affordable reclaimed flooring.

GREENHOMESFORSALE.COM

Greenhomesforsale.com lists available properties across the United States with eco-credentials such as geothermal heating or solar power that are offered directly by homeowners and real estate brokers. You can search listings by fields such as location, home size, number of bedrooms and bathrooms, and price.

JETSON GREEN

Jetsongreen.com

A top destination for following trends in the fast-moving green building industry, Jetson Green is run by Preston Koerner, who makes it his personal mission to keep readers updated on new green building projects, products, technologies, and materials.

THE LAZY ENVIRONMENTALIST

Lazyenvironmentalist.com/homes

I've created a special page to keep Lazy Environmentalist readers updated about ongoing developments in green real estate and home remodeling. Stay on top of emerging trends, materials and new product introductions in the fast-paced, green building industry.

LISTED GREEN

Listedgreen.com

Listed Green lists green apartments, condos, and houses that are available for sale. You can view all listings at once or narrow your search by entering keywords like "solar" or "Energy Star" or entering a city, state, or country. Most listings are for homes in the United States, although there are a few homes listed in Canada and overseas.

MODERN GREEN LIVING

Moderngreenliving.com

Modern Green Living features listings of green residential condos and apartment buildings as well as green neighborhood housing developments throughout the United States and Canada. You can also find local green realtors and other green professionals like interior designers, architects, builders, and general contractors.

NATIONAL ASSOCIATION OF HOME BUILDERS

Nahbgreen.org

The NAHB is the largest home building trade association in the United States, and it's now using its clout to make green building practices more widely adopted among its members. Visit the site to learn about the initiatives under way. You'll also be able to search its online database of local green building programs throughout the country, which is an excellent way to find green homes and green builders in your area.

REGREEN

Regreenprogram.org

Discover best practices and case studies of outstanding green design home remodeling projects at this website developed in partnership between American Society of Interior Designers and the U.S. Green Building Council. Regreen is a wonderful resource to consult when looking for ideas to give your home an eco-makeover.

U.S. GREEN BUILDING COUNCIL

Usgbc.org

The driving force behind today's green building boom, the USGBC has established its LEED (Leadership in Environmental and Energy Design) certification as the most widely adopted green building standard covering all types of buildings, from residential apartment buildings to single-family homes. LEED for neighborhood development encourages the growth of residential developments that reduce sprawl, foster a sense of community, and lower the collective eco-impact of all residents.

WALK SCORE

Walkscore.com

Use Walk Score to quickly find a walkable place to live. Just type in a zip code and Walk Score will return a score (0 to 100 with 100 being most walkable) that indicates walkability to nearby stores, restaurants, schools, parks, and other amenities. Ditch the car and find a cool community where walking is practical and enjoyable.

7

Eco at Home
Sustainable
Furnishings
+ a Greener
Garden

Going green at home (on a budget) is easier than ever.
As fashion designers continue to implement eco-friendly fabric into stylish clothing, designers of home furnishings and accessories are also transforming earth-conscious materials into irresistible gear for every room in the house. You may not be able to give your place a complete green overhaul, but every bit counts. You can start here.

MAKE AN ORGANIC BED

The desire for a greener bedroom has created some unique partnerships. Bed, Bath & Beyond, the giant home goods retailer, has teamed up with Clodagh, one of the world's leading interior designers (according to magazines like *Architectural Digest* and *Robb Report*). Clodagh's design genius has transformed the W Hotel in Fort Lauderdale and the prestigious Sasanqua Spa at Kiawah Island off the coast of South Carolina, and with the help of Bed, Bath & Beyond, your own home may be next. Available exclusively at B, B & B, the Clodagh for Homestead collection features organic cotton duvets, shams, and accent pillows available in colors White Clay, Red Earth, Deep Sea, or Irish Moss. Duvets start at $149.99 for a twin and run to $179.99 for a king; shams range between $49.99 and $59.99; and pillows are $44.99. Organic cotton sheets and towels are also in development.

Round out your eco-bedroom with other finds available exclusively from Bed, Bath & Beyond. Start with Eco Luxe 300-thread-count organic cotton mattress pads ($49.99 to $89.99) and cover them with Simply Organic 230-thread-count organic cotton flannel or sateen sheet sets ($39.99 and $79.99). You can also pick up comparably priced organic cotton herringbone blankets tinted with colorful low-impact dyes. Pillows have also received an eco-upgrade. Rest your head on pillows stuffed with recycled fiber and covered in 300-thread-count organic cotton for just $19.99. B, B & B's also got you covered in the bathroom. Deliciously soft organic cotton bath towels sell for $14.99. Hand towels are $10.99, and washcloths are just $6.99. Choose from eight different shades of blue, green, brown, or white.

Bed, Bath & Beyond may be making good green design more affordable and accessible, but at Wal-Mart it is unbelievably inexpensive. Organic cotton sheet sets—300-thread-count, no skimping here—range between $29.88 and $39.88. The natural color palette—look for several shades of gray as well as white and green—easily blends with most interiors. Wal-Mart is also turning ingeo, a renewable fiber made from the byproducts of corn, into affordable comforters and mattress pads. The soft mattress pads range between $44.88 and $69.88 while comforters are between $49.88 and $79.88. Wal-Mart organic cotton towel sets are available at prices that boggle the eco-friendly imagination. Available in a variety of colors, a complete organic cotton towel set—including a bath towel, hand towel, and washcloth—will set you back just $14.99.

West Elm, Target, J.C. Penney, Gaiam, Crate & Barrel, and Pottery Barn are also in on the organic cotton bed and bath trend. Here's a hint: Turn to Pottery Barn Teen at Pbteen.com for whimsical patterns that will also please those over 20. The Fresh Flower organic cotton sheet sets start at $79.99 for a twin bed and go up to $129 for a queen. And Eco-Stripe's narrow rows of red, brown, green, yellow, and white create a warm, modern feel on any bed (also available at Pbteen.com).

Bamboo is also a plush bedding or towel option for budget-minded Lazy Environmentalists. Made from the fibers of rapidly growing bamboo stalks, which can reach heights up to 100 feet (with no pesticides or insecticides), bamboo fiber is a soft, silky eco-option. As you seek out bamboo items, be aware of retailers who use "bamboo" in the product name even when bamboo comprises less than 50 percent of the fabric used. Take a minute to closely read product labels to discover just how much bamboo is actually being used. For 100 percent bamboo sheets that start at $49.99 for a twin set and go up to $99.99 for a king set, head back to Bed, Bath & Beyond. A stroll down the towel aisle will lead you to elegantly embroidered products from Lenox that are 70 percent bamboo and 30 percent conventional cotton ($9.99 for a hand towel and up to $24.99 for a bath towel). While not 100 percent eco-optimal, Lenox towels are substantively better for the planet than the standard choice and therefore Lazy Environmentalist endorsed. Other bamboo options are available from Mad Mod (Mad-mod.com), a modern lifestyle store based in Nashville, Tennessee. Look for 100 percent bamboo towel sets for $26 and a set of three 100 percent bamboo kitchen towels for $24.95.

SET A GREEN TABLE

Begin your affordable eco-kitchen odyssey with a selection of contemporary recycled glassware courtesy of Luigi Bormioli. Founded in Parma, Italy, in 1946, the family-run business today is one of Italy's most prominent glassmakers, and the company's Green collection will lend your table an air of sophisticated Italian eco-chic. Purchase a set of 13-ounce tumblers, 18-ounce beverage glasses, or 20-ounce goblets ($17.99 for a 4-set). An 84-ounce pitcher is also just $17.99, as is a three-section serving dish and a two-bowl chip and dip set. You can find the entire collection at Target.

Eco-retailer Green Feet (Greenfeet.com) can set you up with recycled glass drinking glasses ($2.75 each), mugs ($3.95 each), and tumblers ($4.95 each) as well as tapered vases and candle holders (both $4.95). Don't forget to pick up elegant recycled glass bowls and plates for about $8 each. Bluehouse, a Baltimore-based green design store, features La Mediterranea, a collection of modern recycled glassware imported from Spain. Oenophiles as well as casual wine fans will appreciate the slouchy, asymmetrical decanter for $30. Pair it with the round-mouthed tumblers ($4 each) to achieve a contemporary tapas-bar vibe. Crank up the flamenco music, and you'll be all set.

Other recycled materials can help you set a cost-friendly yet colorful tabletop. The Preserve collection of tableware features dishwasher-safe, 100 percent recycled plastic plates, 16-ounce cups, and cutlery available in vibrant red, green, blue hues. Nearly all of the recycled plastic starts its life as Stonyfield yogurt cups before being transformed into affordable tableware. Pick up an 8-pack of large plates for $7. A 10-pack of cups sells for $5.99. And a 24-count canister of knives, forks, and spoons is available for $5.50. Cutting boards have also been introduced using Paperstone, a hard, durable surface material created from 100 percent recycled paper. You can purchase them ($12.99 to $24.99) and most other Preserve products directly at Recycline.com. While you're there, also check out the ergonomically designed Preserve toothbrushes and razors constructed from recycled plastic. They come with pre-paid return envelopes so you can mail them back to the company for additional recycling when you're ready for a new brush or razor. If you misplace the envelope, you can always print a pre-paid label directly from Preserve's website—talk about easy recycling! In 2008, the Preserve collection also expanded to include bright, colorful colanders, cutting boards, and food storage containers made from recycled plastic. A new Preserve program with Brita now recycles the plastic from Brita pitcher filters for use in its collection, too.

Bamboo also plays a key role in an eco-inspired kitchen. The plant's sturdy reeds can be pressed together to form rigid boards that can then be crafted into fine products for the home. Target and Bed, Bath & Beyond are the co-champions of the affordable bamboo kitchen. Both offer popular bamboo items like cutting boards, blocks for knife sets, serving and cutlery trays, serving bowls and utensils, spice racks, and salt and pepper mills ranging from less than $10 to around $50 for individual items. You can also pick up bamboo napkin holders and paper towel holders for around $10 each at both stores. But Target pulls in front with several bamboo items that deserve special recognition, like the Ginsu Santoku 3-piece Knife and Cutting Board Set ($19.99); the curvy bamboo banana hanger ($9.99); the cutting board with built-in slicer ($19.99); and the Chefmate 7-piece BBQ set (including basting brush, barbecue fork, barbecue skewer, barbecue tongs, slotted turner, and cleaning brush) made of bamboo and stainless steel ($19.99). While you're outfitting the kitchen in bamboo, don't forget the bathroom. Target sells a variety of bamboo gear for the washroom including tissue and toothbrush holders, wastebaskets, lotion dispensers, and soap dishes. Prices start around $9 for individual items and go up to $40.

To dress your dining table, turn to Mio Culture, a dynamic, Philadelphia, Pennsylvania–based eco-design firm. The company's Haute Surface Sets ($19.99 each) are made of rapidly renewable cork pieces that can be configured as place mats, protective surfaces for hot serving dishes or table runners. Each set consists of 12 pieces six tan and six chocolate—and resemble jigsaw puzzle pieces that can be assembled however you choose.

Even your oven mitts, dishcloths, pot holders, and kitchen towels can go eco. Visit Bed, Bath & Beyond for a complete set made from organic cotton and low-impact dyes ($26).

FURNISH SUSTAINABLY

Designers and entrepreneurs are continually crafting beautiful furniture out of environmentally responsible materials, but these collections are rarely inexpensively priced. The hefty price tags are due to a simple but frustrating fact: Small companies are unable to manufacture enough products to reduce costs in ways that larger companies can. However, a few smaller companies have found their way around this issue while larger companies are also beginning to add affordably priced, well-designed eco-friendly furniture to their inventories. And when shopping for environmentally conscious furniture, you'll find that it can be made from reclaimed and recycled materials, rapidly renewable materials (like bamboo), or wood that has been harvested from forests that are responsibly managed.

The South Shore collection of TV stands, desks, and bedroom furniture is ideal for Lazy Environmentalists on a budget. The amazingly affordable laminated wood furniture is made of composite wood panels created entirely from recovered and recycled

Eric Hudson is founder and CEO of Recycline, a company that makes contemporary household items using recycled plastic.

How did you get the idea for Recycline?
It all started with a toothbrush. Back when it wasn't easy being a greenie, I decided to combine my career and my love of nature by creating a company that I felt good coming to every day. I set out to invent an innovative version of an everyday item and address a functional challenge that I thought possible to improve on. The tooth-brush, a product that everyone used—at least we all hope—was the object of my desire. Could a toothbrush be made from recycled materials? Only time would tell. The first Preserve Toothbrush was born, and at the time, when recycled material offerings were scarce in the marketplace, and higher quality ones nonexistent, the toothbrush was a hit, and converts flocked to Recycline's flagship product. That was in 1996, and we have been growing ever since.

What is Recycline's positive environmental impact?
At Recycline, environmental stewardship is the coursing blood running through our individual and corporate actions. We are constantly look-ing to improve our positive environmental impact in every area of our products and operations. We use recycled and environment-friendly materials for all of our products and packaging. We do not use toxic, harmful chemicals, and we never test on animals. Our offices run on clean energy. Most of our employees bike, train, or walk to work, and we seek to make our products regionally to reduce transportation costs. Our hope is that when people see how easy it is to replace a traditional toothbrush with our high-performance, eco-friendly Preserve toothbrush, they will begin to wonder what other easy steps they can take to live a more sustainable lifestyle.

materials. While panels like these are often sealed with urea-formaldehyde (a carcinogenic chemical) glues, South Shore meets California's stringent limits on formaldehyde emissions from composite wood products like plywood, particleboard, and MDF (medium density fiberboard). Though such emissions have been regulated throughout Europe, Japan, and Australia for some time, California implemented the first U.S. restrictions in early 2009. As for South Shore's products, you'll find contemporary, traditional, and sleek modern TV stands for under $200; full entertainment centers, including TV stand and two bookcases, for under $600; and computer desks starting below $200. Kids of all ages will love the Latté two-tone cream and walnut platform bed with bookcase headboard available in a twin size for $434.99 ($10 more gets you the full size). The bed features a convenient storage drawer for bedding, off-season clothes, or nonclaustrophobic stuffed animals. For a contemporary East-meets-West look, look for South Shore's Bali bedroom collection. The queen-sized platform bed and headboard are available for just $339.99; the nightstands are $122.99 each; and the chests and dressers sell for around $200 each. Find great deals on all styles at Elegantsouthshore.com and Southshorecentral.com; many retailers including Sears carry the products in-store for in-person viewing.

Outfit your home affordably with furniture made from FSC (Forest Stewardship Council) certified wood through Indianapolis, Indiana–based InModern. The FSC label ensures that wood products have come from a responsibly managed forest. While InModern's furniture collections help you make a smarter planetary purchase, you'll also appreciate its contemporary styles of desks, coffee tables, end tables, occasional tables, stools, storage centers, entertainment centers, and magazine racks. InModern's Rekindle and Intown collections evoke the modernist sentiments of the mid-twentieth century, while the angular lines of the Linear collection combine style and utility. The Surfin line adds a touch of whimsy with softer fluid shapes. Whatever your style, you'll appreciate the company's patented "slot together" assembly requiring no nuts, bolts, or tools of any kind. Desks sell for $420. Coffee tables are $360. The most expensive piece you'll find is the Linear Shelving + Storage, available for $720. Pair it with a magazine rack for an extra $60. All furniture is made in the United States and finished with nontoxic, water-based stains. Target carries the line as do online modern furniture shops like 2Modern.com and DesignPublic.com.

For serious eco-lounging on a budget, check out Wal-Mart's Tre Bamboo Chair and Ottoman Set ($299.95). Constructed using nontoxic, water-based glues and finishes and styled after the Eames designs of the mid-century modern movement, the curved chair and ottoman are proof that good green design can be affordable for the masses. You can also turn to Wal-Mart to meet your outdoor needs with eco-smart furniture fit for the porch, patio, or deck. An FSC-certified wood outdoor dining set is available for $468 and includes a table, four chairs, and a two-seat bench (assembly is required, which helps keeps prices low—really low). The sleek FSC-certified wood Delahey Sun Lounger chaise lounge can be adjusted at the back, arms, and feet and features a fold-out shelf and wheels for rolling it in and out of the shade ($138). Other FSC items include an Espresso Dining set with a 72-inch-long table, two side benches, and two end chairs for $398. The heavy-duty Cambridge Rectangular Dining Table ($234) is made from yellow balau wood in an updated arts and crafts style. Balau is naturally water repellant and with proper treatment will last many seasons. This table is so nice that you might even consider bringing it indoors. Matching dining chairs are available for $64 each. After your big meal, kick back in the Unique Arts Outdoor Relaxing

Chair, available for $52. The foldable, portable chair is also made
of yellow balau wood and will withstand the elements while delivering plenty of comfort. Many other FSC-certified items are also
available. Start your search at Walmart.com/earth.

HOW GREEN IS YOUR GARDEN: LANDSCAPING AND GARDENING

Looking to organically care for your lawn or grow your garden?
There's an easy way to start: Test your soil. When you use synthetic chemicals to treat your lawn and garden, they can seep into
the groundwater—and into you, your kids, your pets, and anyone
else who decides to play outside. But before you dive into natural organic fertilizers, plant foods, pesticides, and herbicides, it's
essential to learn about your soil so you can choose the right products to optimize it. Nutrient-rich and well-balanced soil—not too
acidic or alkaline—is the starting point for greening your green
thumb. You can hire a local soil-testing professional or you can visit
PlanetNatural.com to purchase a do-it-yourself kit for under $20.
Once you know where your soil stands, you'll be prepared to make
the transition to organic.

Many respected companies specializing in natural organic lawn
and gardening products were founded in the years BG, that is, in
the years Before Gore. These were the years before *An Inconvenient
Truth* and before the green living movement began to gain widespread cultural acceptance. These companies have had decades to
develop effective and affordable solutions. But there are also recent
standouts to the organic landscape scene like TerraCycle, a young
company that shows us how discarded waste can be transformed
into some of the finest and most affordable garden products available. Whatever eco-wise gardening company you turn to, there's
no time like the present to make the switch.

One of the oldest manufacturers of affordable natural organic
landscaping products is Espoma, founded in Millville, New Jersey,
in 1929. The company became famous throughout the gardening
industry for the organic plant food it first developed for hollies,
azaleas, rhododendrons, and other plants that thrive in acidic soil.
Aptly named Holly-Tone, the plant food is still a favorite among gar-

Fritz Haeg is founder and lead garden designer of Edible Estates, an ongoing series of projects to replace the American front lawn with edible garden landscapes.

How did you get the idea for Edible Estates?

I wanted to do a project that dealt with how we are living collectively as Americans today. It struck me that the front lawn is one thing we all have in common. It's a space that we all collectively tend and appreciate together and cuts across economic, political, religious, racial, geographic, and regional boundaries. Here was a piece of land that was ready for reconsideration, and if we all reconsidered it together, that would be really powerful. And growing food there seemed to be a very natural thing to do and something that I had been experimenting with on my own property. Of course, there is nothing remotely new about this idea. That is one part of the project that strikes me as rather funny—to take an activity that is so basic and naturally human, which we have become alienated from, and then reposition it for contemporary culture. Giving it the name Edible Estates was an important aspect of creating an identity for this front lawn alternative.

What is Edible Estate's positive environmental impact?

The front lawn represents a real wasted opportunity, a vast amount of visible land that we have claimed but do not occupy, that we also cover with chemicals, rarely pour fresh water on, pollute with our mowers . . . and then it even isolates us from our neighbors. By growing food there, we take a wasteful, polluting, isolating space and transform it into a healthy, productive, connecting space. The food we grow there is as local as you can get, reducing the amount of food that is shipped around the world and reducing our dependence on pesticides that are required for an industrial monoculture.

At what point does the neighborhood stop freaking out?
After the first few weeks of growth, neighbors that were resistant to the garden start to warm up to it. When you have an Edible Estate, you are probably in front of your house every day doing a bit of gardening. I think we identify and empathize with people that put that much care into anything, especially a garden that is growing every day in front of our eyes. Perhaps for some, eating that first fresh tomato from the neighbor's garden is when they stop freaking out and really get it.

deners. You can pick up a 5-pound bag for about $5—a 50-pound bag sells for just over $21—at True Value Hardware. Espoma makes Plant-Tone and Garden-Tone as well as products dedicated to achieving the optimum soil pH level for specific flowers (Rose-Tone) or vegetables (Tomato-Tone). Espoma also makes natural pesticides and organic lawn foods. A store finder on the company's website will help you quickly locate a retailer near you.

Based in Orange, Virginia, St. Gabriel Organics has been creating highly effective organic insecticides, pesticides, and herbicides since 1986. The company's initial goal was to tame the havoc-wreaking Japanese beetle. The all-natural Milky Spore insecticide infects the white grubs of Japanese beetles with milky spore disease, a naturally occurring bacterium that's bad for Japanese beetles but safe for other beneficial insects and the environment. A 10-ounce can sells for $24.50 at PlanetNatural.com and can treat a 2,500-square-foot area. If you've got moles or voles that also feed on grubs, then combine Milky Spore with St. Gabriel Organics' Holy Moley, a nontoxic and nonpoisonous substance that tastes nasty enough for rodents to feed elsewhere. A 10-pound bag costs $17.99, can treat an area up to 5,000 square feet, and is available through the company's own shopping site (Stgl.us). St. Gabriel Organics is also attracting fans with its BurnOut Weed & Grass Killer, a potent combination of clove oil, lemon juices, and vinegar that takes down weeds and unwanted grass ($7.95 for a 24-ounce bottle, also at PlanetNatural.com). Dining alfresco? Then you'll love the company's Natural Mosquito Repellant that turns garlic juice, citronella, white pepper, potassium sorbate, and molasses into a nasty cocktail that not only repels mosquitoes but also gnats, fleas, and ticks. Repellant will clear an area of about 5,000 square feet for two to four weeks. A 32-ounce bottle with a hose-end sprayer is available from BackyardStyle.com for $15.39.

While companies like Espoma and St. Gabriel Organics have been rocking the natural and organic backyard for some time, the green gardening movement—and the green movement in general—is gaining greater recognition through the work of TerraCycle. Here's how it works: Hire a billion worms to munch on food waste in a factory in Trenton, New Jersey, collect the resulting mounds of worm poop, package it in reused plastic bottles and jugs, and then ship it to mega-retailers like Home Depot and Wal-Mart, where the resulting fertilizers and plant foods are sold at prices competitive with conventional products. Through this process, TerraCycle provides high-quality, affordable, eco-friendly products while keeping thousands of tons of waste out of landfills. It gets better: TerraCycle partners with schools and other institutions throughout the United States to form "Bottle Brigades." The Brigades get paid to collect their own used bottles and ship them to TerraCycle's facility, where they are turned into packaging. The program is an ingenuous way for TerraCycle to build a broad network of trash collectors while simultaneously encouraging children to take responsibility for their own waste and providing them with an opportunity to effect environmental change. Additional Brigades are under way as TerraCycle expands into product categories like office supplies, bags, and cleaning products (see Chapter 1: The 3Rs and Chapter 8: A Greener Way to Clean for more on TerraCycle's products). In the meantime, purchase a gallon of TerraCycle All-Purpose Plant Fertilizer packaged in a used milk jug for $9.99 at Home Depot or Wal-Mart. Or visit Gardeners.com to find 20-ounce bottles of Orchid, African Violet, or All-Purpose Plant Food ($6.95 each) packaged in reused Pepsi soda bottles. TerraCycle has also recently partnered with the Kendall-Jackson winery to transform used oak wine barrels into rain barrels to collect water from your roof and composters to turn your lawn clippings, leaves, and other yard waste into natural fertilizer. Both products retail for $99 at Sam's Club as well as gardening centers around the country.

A growing frustration among many Lazy Environmentalists is the expensive price of organic foods. As much as we want to feed our bodies healthier products while doing our part for the planet, we don't always have the financial resources to make that choice. One way to counter the high cost is grow your own organic produce. The companies mentioned above can help make that possible. You'll also want to keep a copy of *Grow Organic* by Doug Oster and Jessica Walliser by your side. The book provides practical, doable advice and more than 250 tips for newbie gardeners and veterans alike. Oster and Walliser also co-host their own radio show, *The Organic Gardeners,* and are frequent writers and guest lecturers around the United States. Jump start your organic gardening efforts by learning from their expertise and experience. And even if you don't have space for an outdoor garden, you can consider bringing your garden indoors. *Grow Organic* has suggestions, and Cleanairgardensupply.com has affordable planters for growing everything from tomatoes to asparagus inside your own home.

Organic gardening may seem more "environmentalist" than "lazy," but that was before Wal-Mart got in on the game. The world's largest retailer is soon to become the largest retailer of organic produce. Using its massive purchasing power to lower the costs of organic produce, Wal-Mart provides a welcome opportunity to eat healthier and support organic farming around the globe. Some may take issue with the fact that Wal-Mart's produce must often be shipped thousands of miles to reach its stores, resulting in lots of greenhouse gas emissions. Or people may complain that Wal-Mart's low prices will drive small, organic family farms out of business. There's credence to these arguments. But from the Lazy Environmentalist's perspective, Wal-Mart's entry into organic produce is a significantly better choice than the conventional option— purchasing low-priced produce that's both nonorganic and shipped from thousands of miles away. We can opt to embrace self-reliance by growing our own organic food, we can support our local organic farms by shopping at farmers' markets and other locations where their food is sold, or we can cruise the aisles of Wal-Mart to purchase the lowest priced organic food around. In their own unique way, each of these choices supports a Lazy Environmentalist lifestyle by being better for your health and better for the planet.

Furniture and Furnishings

BEANBAGBLITZ.COM
Sit in eco-comfort with a recycled beanbag chair from Beanbagblitz.com. Stuffed with nontoxic recycled polystyrene beads and covered in Eco Suede fabric made from recycled soda bottles, the Recycle Integra Eco Chair ($79.99) will provide plenty of comfort and support for gaming sessions or Netflix night.

CLODAGH
Clodagh.com
Clodagh has teamed up with Bed, Bath & Beyond to offer the Clodagh for Homestead bedding collection featuring organic cotton duvets, shams, and accent pillows available in colors White Clay, Red Earth, Deep Sea, or Irish Moss. Duvets start at $149.99 for a twin and run to $179.99 for a king; shams range between $49.99 and $59.99; and pillows are $44.99.

INMODERN
Inmodern.net
Purchase affordable, FSC-certified wood furniture from this Indianapolis, Indiana–based green design company. Contemporary-style desks, coffee tables, end tables, occasional tables, stools, storage centers, entertainment centers, and magazine racks are all on offer for prices that range from $60 for a magazine rack to $720 for a bookcase.

LUIGI BORMIOLI
Luigibormioli.com
Founded in Parma, Italy, in 1946, Luigi Bormioli is one of Italy's most prominent glassmakers. The company's contemporary Green collection, made of recycled glass, includes tumblers, beverage glasses, and goblets as well as pitchers, serving dishes, and bowls. You can find the items at Bed, Bath & Beyond, Target, and Amazon.com for less than $25 each.

MIO CULTURE

Mioculture.com

This Philadelphia, Pennsylvania–based eco-design firm will help you set a stylish green table thanks to its Haute Surface Sets ($19.99 each). They're made of rapidly renewable cork pieces that can be configured as place mats, protective surfaces for hot serving dishes, or table runners. Each set consist of 12 pieces—six tan and six chocolate—and resemble jigsaw puzzle pieces that can be assembled however you choose.

PRESERVE

Recycline.com

The Waltham, Massachusetts–based company has partnered with Stonyfield Farm to turn its yogurt cups—from organic yogurt, of course—into affordable and ergonomic recycled plastic toothbrushes, razors, and colorful kitchenware. Find dishwasher-safe, 100 percent recycled plastic cups, cutlery, plates, cutting boards, colanders, and storage containers. A new Preserve program with Brita now recycles the plastic from Brita pitcher filters for use in its collection too.

SOUTH SHORE FURNITURE

Southshorefurniture.com

Style-conscious, budget-conscious, and eco-conscious is the Lazy Environmentalist trifecta, and South Shore Furniture delivers on all three with products made of composite wood panels created entirely from recovered and recycled materials. You'll find contemporary, traditional, and sleek modern TV stands for under $200, full entertainment centers for under $600, and computer desks starting below $200.

TRADERS AND COMPANY

Tradersandcompany.net

This retailer of imported home décor and giftware offers an extensive selection of affordably priced recycled glass kitchen- and tableware. Vases come in all shapes and sizes and start at around $20. A 64-ounce pitcher is $22 and a textured 16-inch 3-section serving dish is $28.

Landscaping and Gardening

ESPOMA

Espoma.com

Espoma became famous throughout the gardening industry for the organic plant food it first developed for hollies, azaleas, rhododendrons, and other plants that thrive in acidic soil. Aptly named Holly-Tone, the plant food is still a favorite among gardeners. Also look for Plant-Tone and Garden-Tone as well as products dedicated to achieving the optimum soil pH level for specific flowers (Rose-Tone) or vegetables (Tomato-Tone).

ST. GABRIEL ORGANICS
Milkyspore.com
St. Gabriel Organics has been creating highly effective organic insecticides, pesticides, and herbicides since 1986. The company's signature Milky Spore insecticide neutralizes the Japanese beetle. St. Gabriel Organics is also attracting fans with its BurnOut Weed & Grass Killer, a potent combination of clove oil, lemon juices, and vinegar that takes down weeds and unwanted grass.

TERRACYCLE
Terracycle.net
TerraCycle is redefining America's relationship with its trash. The company's highly acclaimed natural plant foods are made from worm poop, packaged in empty Pepsi bottles, and sold at affordable prices at retail giants like Wal-Mart and Home Depot. Look for TerraCycle rain barrels and composters made from used Kendall-Jackson oak wine barrels, available at Sam's club and garden centers around the country for $99.

Retailers

BED, BATH & BEYOND
If you're looking for affordable, comfortable, and super-stylish organic cotton and bamboo bedding and bath products or a wide range of bamboo kitchen furnishings, Bed, Bath & Beyond can deliver the goods. You'll be pleasantly surprised at the range of eco-products available for less than $100. Or splurge on the Clodagh for Homestead organic bedding collection, with prices that range between $49.99 and $179.99.

BLUEHOUSE
Bluehouselife.com
A Baltimore-based green design store, Bluehouse features the La Mediterranea collection of modern recycled glassware imported from Spain. Oenophiles as well as casual wine fans will appreciate the slouchy, asymmetrical decanter for $30. Pair it with the round-mouthed tumblers ($4 each) to achieve a contemporary tapas-bar vibe.

CLEAN AIR GARDENING

Cleanairgardening.com

Start your search here for affordable rain barrels, electric-powered lawn mowers, and everything else you need to create a water- and energy-efficient garden. You can also purchase affordable natural organic lawn and gardening supplies.

GREEN FEET

Greenfeet.com

Eco-retailer Green Feet can set you up with recycled glass drinking glasses ($2.75 each), mugs ($3.95 each), and tumblers ($4.95 each) as well as tapered vases and candle holders (both $4.95). Also check out the full line of bamboo kitchenware and tableware from Bambu.

MAD MOD

Mad-mod.com

This modern lifestyle store is a great source for bamboo bath and bedding products. One hundred percent bamboo towel sets are available for $26, and a set of three 100 percent bamboo kitchen towels sells for $24.95. You can also purchase a comfy, queen-size, 100 percent bamboo blanket for $99.99. Products are also available directly through the company's website.

PLANET NATURAL

Planetnatural.com

This online retailer offers a diverse selection of earth-friendly products for your home, lawn, and garden at affordable prices. The website's resource section contains gardening articles on introductory topics like "Using Organic Fertilizers" and "Changing the pH of Your Soil" as well as more esoteric topics like "The Benefits of Mycorrhizal Fungi" and "The Benefits of Seaweed."

POTTERY BARN TEEN

Pbteen.com

Turn to Pottery Barn Teen for whimsical patterns that will also please the over-20 set. The Fresh Flower organic cotton sheet sets start at $79.99 for a twin bed and go up to $129 for a queen.

TARGET

Target.com

This mega-retailer offers a broad selection of affordable eco-furnishings like the Luigi Bormioli collection of recycled glassware and its own collection of recycled melamine, dishwasher-safe plates, bowls, and cups. And be sure to check out the extensive inventory of affordable bamboo kitchen and bathroom accessories.

WAL-MART
Walmart.com/earth
Wal-Mart is redefining affordable eco-chic with its Tre Bamboo Lounge and Ottoman Set, made of rapidly renewable bamboo for $299.95. The retailer also offers one of the largest collections of FSC-certified outdoor furniture at truly unbeatable prices. You'll also find deals on organic cotton bedding and towels. It's good for Wal-Mart's bottom line, the planet's bottom line, and your bottom line.

Information / Education

EDIBLE ESTATES
Edibleestates.org
Edible Estates is an ongoing series of projects working to replace the American front lawn with edible garden landscapes. Founder Fritz Haeg conceived Edible Estates as a way to more efficiently use our land and natural resources and restore a shared sense of connectedness and community to neighborhoods throughout the United States.

GROW ORGANIC
Theorganicgardeners.com
This book by Doug Oster and Jessica Walliser is an excellent companion for newbie organic gardeners and veterans alike. The book provides practical, doable advice and more than 250 tips to get you started and keep you planting for many seasons to come.

THE LAZY ENVIRONMENTALIST
Lazyenvironmentalist.com/furnish
I've created a special page to keep Lazy Environmentalist readers updated about ongoing developments in green furnishings and gardening products. Gather new ideas for decorating your home in affordable eco-style and embracing your budget-friendly green thumb.

8

A Greener Way to Clean

Nontoxic
Cleaning
Supplies

Lazy Environmentalists want to clean green. We know that wiping down the kitchen counter with a cleaning solution that contains toxic chemicals is counterintuitive (food often touches kitchen counters; chemicals are not good to eat). We refuse to remove the grime from our windows—or toilets or bathtubs or refrigerator shelves—with harsh cleansers. And we won't wash our clothes in the sudsy foam of synthetic detergents. Happily, there are alternatives. Green cleaning products are made from naturally renewable, nontoxic, biodegradable ingredients. They allow you to wipe away grease, grime, dirt, and dust without synthetic chemical cleaners that can degrade indoor air quality, interrupt normal body functioning, seep into groundwater, and erode healthy ecosystems. The best ones successfully clean without most, if not all, of the potentially harmful chemicals found in most conventional cleaners.

While you can whip up a batch of all-purpose, supremely efficient DIY cleanser—mix equal parts water and white vinegar in a spray bottle—sometimes you're looking for a little more oomph in your cleaning. Today, that little oomph is an affordable purchase that's easy to come by. You can find green cleaning products just about everywhere you shop. From big box retailers like Wal-Mart and Target, supermarkets like Food Lion and Safeway, and drug store chains like CVS and Duane Reade, greenness is now all about convenience.

CLEAN THE HOUSE

In 2008, green cleaning welcomed a new product line with a familiar name. Green Works by Clorox tapped into the company's extensive research and development resources to develop a line of products made of natural plant-based, biodegradable ingredients like corn, coconut, and lemon. Green Works features all-purpose cleaning products, glass and mirror sprays, bathroom and toilet bowl cleaners, as well as dish soaps that have repeatedly performed as well or better than conventional products in blind at-home and laboratory tests. The products are never tested on animals and are packaged in plastic recyclable bottles made with at least 25 percent recycled content. Look for Green Works products at Wal-Mart, Sam's Club, and thousands of other locations around the United States. At around $3 per bottle, they're worth putting on your shopping list.

Green cleaning products that are effective, affordable, and available everywhere is an eco-trifecta that this Lazy Environmentalist fully supports. This is why I've aligned on to be a spokesperson for the Green Works brand. While some environmentalists resist eco-solutions presented by large corporations like Clorox, I'm all for them. When big companies offer a green alternative, they are often accused of jumping on the green bandwagon to make a buck. But from the Lazy Environmentalist's perspective, this green bandwagoning is precisely what we need. Every company, consumer, citizen, and government official must move in a green direction if we are going to successfully restore balance to our lifestyles and the planet. As far as I can tell, Mother Nature doesn't care whether we create positive environmental change because we are morally compelled or whether we do it to save a buck, earn a buck, live a healthier life, look cool, or get lucky. As long as substantive, positive environmental change is happening, it's all good.

Clorox has some significant competition in the green game. Method's design-centric packaging—containing some of the most effective earth-friendly cleaning products—is now made from 100 percent recycled plastic. And the company's Go Naked line ups the eco-ante with all-purpose cleaners and dish detergents that are dye- and perfume-free. The omop is also a personal cleaning favorite. The ergonomically designed mop is like the Swiffer, but updated for people who enjoy good design, a clean planet, and an affordable price. The $30 starter kit includes an omop, a washable microfiber mop pad, three corn-based biodegradable and compostable

Jonathan Propper is founder and CEO of Dropps, an eco-aware laundry detergent company committed to reducing waste of both water and plastic.

How did you get the idea for Dropps?

The story goes back to a cotton mill outside of Philadelphia, Pennsylvania, where I founded a company that developed a patented cotton yarn, which gained recognition when Perry Ellis used it to launch his famed hand-knit cotton sweater line. Along the way, I realized there was a need for a better way to care for cotton (and other) fabrics, so I founded Cot'n Wash, a leading concentrated detergent. Then in 2005, after years of encouragement from my wife, who was tired of pouring and measuring liquid laundry detergent, I reformulated the product as Dropps by removing all of the unnecessary water from the original formula and placing the detergent in premeasured dissolving packs.

What is Dropps's positive environmental impact?

Unlike other green laundry detergents, we focus not just on the contents of the package, but also on the packaging itself. In fact, it takes 292 Dropps stand-up pouches to equal the waste of one laundry detergent jug. This is a simple way to make a positive environmental impact without sacrificing value, convenience, or cleaning power. By offering a low-impact alternative to liquid laundry detergents sold in plastic bottles, coldwater-friendly Dropps is the only liquid laundry detergent that saves water, plastic, and energy.

What happens if I drop my Dropps? Do they break? Will they clean my floor?

If you drop your Dropps, they will not break, but they may bounce or even roll a bit. In fact, bouncing Dropps makes a fun little game—without any waste. You can drop your Dropps on the floor without fear of making a mess, and then toss them right into your laundry machine.

sweeping cloths, and a 14-ounce bottle of nontoxic All-Floor-One-Floor cleaning solution. Target, Costco, Staples, and Safeway are just a few of the many retailers who carry the Method brand.

TerraCycle—maker of all things natural, reclaimed, and recycled—also entered into the natural cleaning products category in 2008. The company's cleaners—all-purpose, window, and bathroom, as well a natural degreaser and drain maintainer and cleaner—derive their cleaning power from the concentrated oils of plants, shrubs, fruits, herbs, and grasses. TerraCycle packages its cleaners in reused soda bottles, helping to make it one of the most affordable and eco-responsible cleaning lines available. All products are biodegradable and fragrance-free and retail for $3.99 for a 1-liter bottle, except for the drain maintainer and cleaner, which comes in a 2-liter bottle for $5.99. Find them nationwide at OfficeMax and Home Depot.

Led by founder, CEO, and green movement luminary Jeffrey Hollender, Seventh Generation also continues to excel in green cleaning. The darling of natural supermarket chains and mom-and-pop grocery stores, Seventh Generation continues to serve its exceptionally loyal following while reaching out to new audiences. Thanks to price-competitive products and widespread distribution at stores such as Walgreens and Duane Reade, everyone can access these incredibly efficient all-natural products. Look for an array of household cleaners, including Wild Orange & Cedar Spice Kitchen Cleaner or Emerald Citrus & Fir Tub & Tile Cleaner—both are typically priced between $4 and $5 for a 32-ounce bottle.

WASH YOUR CLOTHES

Laundry plays a big part in household cleaning, and choosing concentrated laundry detergents in smaller-sized packaging is one of the wiser planetary decisions we can make. Smaller, lightweight products are more convenient to carry. From an environmental perspective, they create less waste and require less fuel to transport. The trick is to remove the water from the product since it's going to be added by the laundry machine anyway. Today, you'll find concentrated laundry detergents from just about every major cleaning brand like Tide, Gain, Wisk, and All. If you're loyal to one of these brands and can't bear the thought of opting for a detergent that's nontoxic and healthier for you and your family, stick with your brand, but go for the concentrated version. If, on the other hand, you're searching for a concentrated, nontoxic detergent that works great, go for brands like Seventh Generation, Method, or other highly regarded ones like ECOS and Bi-O-Kleen.

An alternative laundry choice for Lazy Environmentalists on the go is Dropps, a 6x concentrated detergent that comes in tiny, biodegradable packs, which can be dropped directly in the washing machine. The pack then dissolves and the concentrated solution goes to work on your dirt and grime. One Dropp is all you need for small and medium loads, while two Dropps will handle larger loads. The company sells its products on its own website for $6 for a pack of 20. You can also find them at Wal-Mart.com for about 25 percent off the retail price.

FRESHEN AIR

Lazy Environmentalists are big fans of air fresheners, but we like to scent our homes with products that are phthalate-free (toxic synthetic chemicals used to retain fragrances). According to research conducted by the Natural Resources Defense Council, Febreze Air Effects Air Refresher and Renuzit Subtle Effects both get the job done in phthalate-free fashion, while many other conventional fresheners utilize the chemical.

Another good strategy for freshening indoor air quality is plants. In an ironic twist of eco-fate, a study by NASA found that as homeowners better seal their homes to become more energy efficient, they inadvertently worsen their indoor air quality. When homes are tightly sealed, nasty VOCs—harmful indoor air pollutants—from conventional cleaning products as well as our furniture, paint, and carpets are no longer ventilated through uncaulked cracks in the window frames and wallboards. NASA recommends going green—really green—by placing a plant at every 100 to 120 square feet of living space to clean and negate the effects of all those toxins.

BAG THE TRASH

Take out the garbage the eco-responsible way by opting for Seventh Generation's plastic garbage bags, containing upward of 55 percent recycled content in 13-gallon and 33-gallon sizes. You can pick up them up for under $4 for a box of 20 at Gaiam.com or Amazon. com. BioBag makes 100 percent biodegradable trash bags made from GMO (Genetically Modified Organism)-free certified corn. The ideal bag for composters, you can purchase a 25-pack of 3-gallon bags for $5.69 at Drugstore.com. The 13-gallon and 33-gallon sizes are more pricey, at $6.19 for a box of 12 and $5.19 for a box of 5. While these bags help wean us off our dependence on plastics made from oil, their biodegradability is less relevant when sent to the landfill. Here's a dirty trash secret: Biodegradable products don't biodegrade when tossed in with the regular trash and sent to the landfill. Packed down under so much other garbage, these items lack sufficient access to air, oxygen, and the microorganisms needed for the process to occur. The best way to make sure they biodegrade and return to the earth is to compost them.

USE RECYCLED PAPER

What could be more convenient than disposable paper towels, napkins, tissues, and toilet paper? There's no need (or possibility) to wash them when they get dirty. We just use them once and toss them. And while such items save us time and hassle, chopping down trees so we can easily blow our noses or clean up cereal spills might not be the fate Mother Nature intended for these multitasking oxygen producers (trees also produce oxygen, reduce carbon dioxide emissions, prevent soil erosion, and restore ecosystems). But since we can't imagine living without these staples of modern existence, selecting paper products that reduce our toll on the planet without taking a toll on our sensitive areas is a solid eco-strategy. Look for high-quality products made with high percentages of recycled paper content. Price-competitive products are available from companies like Seventh Generation, Green Forest, Earth First, and Marcal. You'll want to test them for yourself to find the ones that work best for you—though when it comes to toilet paper, Marcal is a cut above the rest. It's made of 100 percent recycled content and is soft on your bottom. Greenhome.com sells it online by the case starting at $30 for 48 rolls. To get really good deals on many of these items, consider joining a warehouse club like Sam's Club or Costco, both of which are increasing their eco-friendly selections. For another budget-friendly online shopping destination, try Drugstore.com. Click the "Green & Natural" tab at the top left corner of the homepage to find household paper products from Green Forest and Seventh Generation.

Household Cleaning and Paper Products

BIOBAG
Biobagusa.com
BioBag offers 100 percent biodegradable trash bags made from GMO-free certified corn. The ideal bag for composters, you can purchase a 25-pack of 3-gallon bags for $5.69 at Drugstore.com. The 13-gallon and 33-gallon sizes are more pricey at $6.19 for a box of 12 and $5.19 for a box of 5.

DROPPS
Dropps.com
Dropps is a 6x concentrated detergent that comes in tiny, biodegradable packs that can be dropped directly in the washing machine. The pack then dissolves and the concentrated solution goes to work on your dirt and grime. One Dropp is all you need for small and medium loads while two Dropps will handle larger loads. Purchase a 20-pack for $6.

GREEN WORKS
Greenworkscleaners.com
Green Works natural cleaning products are made of plant-based, biodegradable ingredients like corn, coconut, and lemon. Choose from all-purpose cleaning products, glass and mirror sprays, bathroom and toilet bowl cleaners, and dish soap that are available nationwide at supermarkets, drugstores, and mass-market retailers.

METHOD

Methodhome.com

Method's design-centric packaging contains some of the most effective earth-friendly cleaning products and is now made from 100 percent recycled plastic. The company's Go Naked line ups the eco-ante with all-purpose cleaners ($6.99) and dish detergents ($5.99) that are dye- and perfume-free.

MARCAL

Marcalpaper.com

Marcal's 100 percent recycled paper products are often a cut above the competition in terms of pricing and quality. According to the company, its recycling efforts save 6,000 trees, 2 million gallons of water, and 140,000 gallons of oil every day.

SEVENTH GENERATION

Seventhgeneration.com

Thanks to price-competitive products and widespread distribution at stores such as Walgreens and Duane Reade, everyone can access Seventh Generation's incredibly efficient all-natural products. Choose natural cleaning products, recycled plastic garbage bags, and tissues, toilet paper, napkins, and paper towels containing recycled content to get your home moving in a greener direction.

TERRACYCLE

Terracycle.net

Makers of all things natural, reclaimed, and recycled, upstart TerraCycle entered into the natural cleaning products category in 2008. The company's all-purpose, window, and bathroom cleaners as well its natural degreaser and drain maintainer and cleaner derive their cleaning power from the concentrated oils of plants, shrubs, fruits, herbs, and grasses. TerraCycle packages its cleaners in reused soda bottles.

Information/Education

THE LAZY ENVIRONMENTALIST

Lazyenvironmentalist.com/cleaning

I've created a special page to keep Lazy Environmentalist readers updated about ongoing developments in healthy, green cleaning products and services. Get the latest on how to stay green, clean and lazy.

9

Better for Baby

Green Gear
for the
Small Set

As parents, we do all we can to ensure that

our offspring grow up healthy and strong and become doctors or lawyers or professional tennis players (or was that just my parents?). Whatever dreams you have for your wee one, little people require a massive amount of gear. Giving him or her a healthy, eco-friendly head start means choosing products made with eco-smart materials that lessen our impact on the planet but are made without synthetic chemicals that are disruptive not only to nature but also to young, vulnerable immune systems. Now it's easier and more affordable than ever to equip your child with bottles, blankets, toys, and clothes that are affordable, eco-friendly, and just plain cool.

OUTFIT YOUR OFFSPRING IN (ECO)STYLE

You don't have to look hard to find the latest in eco-friendly fashion for your young ones. The biggest baby retailers now offer products that are safe for kids, easy on the planet, and cost-conscious. Babies "R" Us leads the pack with the most extensive collection of natural and organic baby products. Blankets, onesies, burp cloths, hooded towels, bibs, and kimonos are all available in organic cotton as well as booties, leggings, dresses, pants, tops, and hats. Organic cotton is ideal for babies because it's grown without the carcinogenic pesticides and insecticides used in standard cotton products. While these toxins kill undesirable pests, they can also contaminate water, harm farm workers, and remain inside the cotton fiber as it is transformed into a blanket or T-shirt for your child. With more than 40 eco-friendly brands, Babies "R" Us makes going natural easy and affordable. Gerber's organic cotton sets (including cap, mittens, and booties) are just $9.99, while Krawlers's organic cotton jeans with padded knees (ideal for babies on the go) are $14.99.

For truly affordable organic baby duds, head to the largest purchaser of organic cotton on the planet: Wal-Mart. That's right, the megastore sells some of the most budget-friendly organic cotton baby goods in the world. Wal-Mart's exclusive George Baby line features a variety of newborn sets. A George Baby organic cotton bodysuit and reversible bib are $7. A three-piece George Baby set featuring an organic cotton bodysuit, matching shorts, and reversible bib retails for $5.92. Or pick up a set of three organic cotton bodysuits for $7.88. Look for other organic cotton clothing products from Gerber, Halo, and Kiddopotamus at Wal-Mart's unbeatable prices. A Gerber four-pack of white, organic cotton onesies will set you back just $8.97.

Target and Kohl's are also big on organic cotton baby gear, but if you prefer to go the Lazy Environmentalist route, stay in your bathrobe and do your eco-baby shopping from the comfort of your couch. Type "organic" into Amazon.com's search function and then click "baby" from the left-hand navigation bar to reveal hundreds of organic styles from reputable brands like Kee-Ka, Skoon, Kate Quinn Organics, and Pixel Organics. Sort the products by price from lowest to highest to find items that fall within your budget.

Fashion-forward tots—and the parents who dress them—can complete their look with Speesees and Chapter One Organics. Speesees creates funky, eye-catching clothing and accessories with organic cotton and low-impact dyes, which help to reduce chemical content. Speesees grows its organic cotton in India, where the fair labor conditions at its factory have been certified by Social Accountability International, an organization that helps ensure the basic human rights of workers around the world. But see for yourself. Visit Speesees.com for photos of the Indian fields where its organic cotton is farmed and the factory where its clothing is made. And while you're there, look for seventies-inspired jumpsuits emblazoned with catchy imagery (dandelions, horses, trees) for $26.

Chapter One Organics also designs modern baby clothing from

100 percent organic cotton and low-impact dyes. The retro patterns on the Groovy Pink and Groovy Green dresses ($38) will help you locate your little girl in a crowd, and the Alphabet Soup onesie ($26) gives young ones a leg up on their ABCs. The prices may be steeper than other organic options, but each piece is intentionally roomy for a longer-lasting fit. And you can feel doubly good about purchasing from Chapter One Organics, as the company manufactures its products in a U.S. factory that provides training programs to women who face significant barriers to employment. One such program takes place at a minimum-security prison in the Midwest and helps the inmates find gainful green jobs when they are released. Companies like Chapter One Organics and Speesees are catalysts for positive change on numerous levels, allowing consumers to dress their children in safe and stylish goods while building a world that is full of hope and economic opportunity.

BUILD A BETTER BED

As with clothing, when searching for organic bedding, start big. The mammoth baby emporium, Babies "R" Us, sells TL Care organic cotton crib sheets ($12.99) sized to fit standard crib and toddler mattresses. TL Care also makes an organic cotton reversible blanket for $12.98 and a contoured changing table cover for $14.99 topped with 100 percent organic cotton velour and backed with a blend of 80 percent cotton and 20 percent polyester. At Babies "R" Us, you'll also find organic cotton crib sheets in an array of colors and patterns from Gerber, Tadpoles, Kids Line, Natures Purest, and Wendy Bellissimo starting at about $12.99. To outfit the entire crib at once, look for Kids Line's Bunny Meadow six-piece bedding set, including a duvet with cover, bumper with cover, valance, dust ruffle, fitted sheet, and diaper stacker ($179). The valance, diaper stacker, and bedding are made of 100 percent organic cotton. While the duvet and bumper are made of polyester, their covers are made of 100 percent organic cotton, so everything that touches your baby's skin remains pure. The gender-neutral natural, sage, and brown colors make a perfect shower gift for the mom-to-be who doesn't know what her baby will be.

Wal-Mart also offers the TL Care organic baby bedding line at comparable prices. You'll find a four-piece organic cotton set for $119.97 that includes a reversible comforter, bumper, fitted crib sheet, and crib skirt. While the beige color may not win many interior decorating points, it wins numerous eco-points for being bleach- and dye-free (beige is cotton's natural color).

As for natural mattresses for your babe, the average price tag hovers around $350. But there are affordable options to be had. Babies "R" Us features the Serta Perfect Balance Mattress by Babi Italia ($179.99). And you can find the No-Compromise Organic Cotton Classic by Naturepedic ($259) at Amazon.com and baby boutiques around the country. Both mattresses utilize a continuous innerspring coil system wrapped in layers of organic cotton to provide firm support. The Serta Perfect Balance has a cover made of waterproof vinyl, which claims to be free of phthalates (chemicals that soften plastic and have been connected to several health complications). While vinyl is far from a perfect planetary choice, the mattress is better than most standard choices, which are typically made of petroleum-based polyurethane foam and treated with fire-retardant chemicals or PBDEs (which have been linked to brain and reproductive-system disorders). While the No-Compromise by Naturepedic makes some eco-compromises—the mattress features a cover made of food-grade, stain-resistant, and waterproof polyethylene, a nontoxic plastic that many consider to be a better alternative to vinyl—it's still a good choice for Lazy Environmentalists on a budget. If you're prepared to spend a little more for the surface on which your baby will, with luck, sleep peacefully through the night, then check out the Until Kara mattress, made entirely of organic cotton and natural wool from organically raised sheep ($349). The mattress's breathable wool core also helps to regulate your baby's temperature by wicking away moisture.

FURNISH WISELY

Furniture for the small set may be increasingly eco-friendly, but it has yet to become affordable. Unless you're willing to spend more than $500 on a crib—in which case there are some seriously cool options—your best bet is to seek out solid wood furniture made from trees that have been responsibly harvested. Unless specifically noted otherwise, avoid furniture made of composite woods like plywood and particleboard, which typically utilize glues with toxins like formaldehyde. Solid wood is a safer bet, and you'll find a range of affordable options at trusty Ikea. The purveyor of Swedish meatballs also serves up contemporary, solid beech wood cribs that start under $100. Ikea purchases its wood from Scandinavia, Eastern Europe, and China, where the company has teamed up with the Rainforest Alliance and the World Wildlife Fund (WWF) to promote responsible forestry management through the Forest Stewardship Council (FSC) certification. The FSC provides one of the most credible, third-party-verified sustainable forestry certifications available. Not all of Ikea's furniture is certified sustainable, but the company continues to implement an environmental program geared toward reaching that goal. As for furniture that does includes composite boards, Ikea claims to use glues that conform to more stringent European standards and are therefore less harmful than those used in the United States. The good news on this side of the ocean is that in early 2009 California implemented the first regulations in the country to reduce the amount of formaldehyde (one of the most noxious offenders) found in composite wood products, an excellent step toward making healthful baby furniture more affordable and more widely available.

GIVE THEM SOMETHING GOOD TO CHEW

If your baby is going to chew, suck, or drool on something, why not make that something as safe as possible? When it comes to bottles, it's best to choose items free from Bisphenol-A (otherwise known as BPA), a chemical used to make hard glass-like plastic that is increasingly suspected of disrupting human hormone systems. Adiri's line of BPA-free Natural Nurser Ultimate Baby Bottles are $12 and feature the unique "Fill, Twist and Feed System," which allows for single-hand preparation. As any parent of an infant knows, being able to tie your shoes, make toast, or prepare a bottle with one hand is key. BornFree also offers a quality line of BPA-free plastic bottles and glass bottles. Pick up a triple-pack of 5-ounce bottles complete with colic-alleviating venting system for $26.99. For an organic, all-natural, BPA-free pacifier, go for Natursutten Pacifiers ($7.95). The "better binkie" is made of pure natural rubber tapped directly from rubber trees. The one-piece design is extremely hygienic and softer than silicone (the most common pacifier material). You'll find them at Zoebonline.com. And visit Nuby for an entire line of colorful, affordable, BPA-free feeding gear, including nursing bottles, sippy cups, utensils, food trays, and storage containers.

PLAY IT SAFE

The right toys provide children with endless of hours of entertainment while expanding their creativity and concentration. The right green toys ensure that they're doing it safely. For budding architects and builders, nontoxic Kapla Blocks open endless building possibilities. The solid pine wood blocks are made in France from sustainably managed forests. The long, thin blocks are of heirloom quality, uniform dimension, and are constructed according to the same 1:3:5 proportions commonly used to form bricks, beams, and planks—optimal for creating complex structures. The 40-piece set retails for $30; the 200-piece set for $69.80. Stack the blocks horizontally to build an impenetrable fort or vertically to build airy pagodas or high-rise towers. Visit Kaplatoys.com to view a picture gallery of the blocks in action.

PlanToys also offers a series of delightful eco-responsible wood toys. The Germany-based company designs enticing rattles, rings, and spin bells, as well as toy caterpillars, cars, teddy bears, and penguins, all for under $15. Older children will love PlanToys's wooden play sets like the Railway, Road, Airport, Crane, Parking Garage, Pirate Ship, and Circus. As with all PlanToys, the sets are made with nontoxic vegetable dyes and the solid wood comes from plantation-grown rubber trees that are harvested after their useful life as rubber producers has run its course. You can also pick up dolls and dollhouses, riding trikes, and other toys suitable for lots of ages.

Rachel Pearson is founder and creative director of Speesees, a children's clothing company committed to being fun, fair, and organic.

How did you get the idea for Speesees?
I became inspired to create comfortable, cute, and high-quality clothing when my friends began giving birth. Named s-p-e-e-s-e-e-s because it's the way a baby might spell "species" if a baby could spell, *Speesees* pays homage to the animal, plant, and human species on our planet.

What is Speesees' positive environmental impact?
Our cotton is 100 percent Skal-certified organic, which means no pesticides or chemical fertilizers have been used in its cultivation. *Speesees* fabrics are treated with low-impact herbal dyes, and our prints are made with pigments that altogether skip harmful chemicals such as PVC, dioxin, and formaldehyde. These efforts are also a way to do our part to help reduce groundwater pollution. Other ways in which our carbon footprint is a wee bit smaller: Here in the United States we use natural sunlight in the offices, encourage nearly the entire staff to take public transportation, and also use recycled paper products for almost everything from toilet paper to product labels.

How common is it for babies to be better dressed than their parents?
Common! Babies can be the vehicle through which parents express their creativity. Though once a little one experiences our buttery-soft cotton, well, he or she is hooked and the style becomes an afterthought.

Switzerland-based Hape has created the first toy collection made from bamboo, a fast-growing, rapidly renewable grass. Developed in collaboration with UNESCO (United Nations Education, Scientific, and Cultural Organization), the line includes the 120-piece Cantina stacking block set, which retails for $18.95. The pieces come in 10 different colors and are perfect for designing bridges, towers, spirals, and other intricate patterns. Pandabo is a stacking game in which players take turns stacking bamboo-like reeds and wood-shaped pieces on top of a panda. It's available for about $12 and is fun for the entire family. Other brain teasers in the collection include the beautifully designed Colora ($20) and Trapecolo ($25) puzzle games, which develop pattern recognition and sequencing skills. The high-quality construction ensures that these games will provide fun for years to come.

For afternoon tea parties, turn to Green Toys. Made from recycled plastic milk jugs free from toxins like BPA and phthalates, the Green Toys Tea Set includes a teapot, sugar bowl, and creamer plus spoons, saucers, and cups for four ($25). Other Green Toys products include the Indoor Gardening Kit, Sand Play Set, and the Cookware & Dining Set. All products are made in the United States.

If your child finds that he or she has some vacancies at that tea party, turn to the organic stuffed characters from miYim. Pure, untreated, unbleached, and unprocessed organic cotton is combined with natural dyes derived from plants and minerals. miYim's stuffed animals are safe, soft, and really good secret keepers. Retailing between $25 and $30, Hugo the dog, Annabelle the sheep, and Chester the bear will turn tea for two into a rollicking tea fiesta. And babies will love miYim's organic cotton blankees, rattles, and crib and stroller toys featuring a veritable safari of animals like giraffes, bunnies, monkeys, chickens, bears, and elephants. Baby accessories retail for about $12.

Budding automotive buffs can learn about alternative energy while assembling a miniature car powered from the sun. The Solar Car Book from Klutz (complete with car) is $20 and filled with fun facts, diagrams, and instructions for constructing and running the eco-friendly vehicle. For a happy, hopping solar-powered frog ($14.25), head to Fatbraintoys.com. The site offers one of the widest selections of eco-friendly toys available today. Click on "Green & Organic Toys" in the left-hand column to view all of the available products. And don't miss ChildTrek.com and Amazon.com/green for even more eco-aware playthings.

CHOOSE GREEN DIAPERS

Lazy Environmentalists looking for an easy and affordable diaper solution can turn to Seventh Generation. A leader in natural household products, Seventh Generation also serves babies with its line of Chlorine Free Diapers, made of wood pulp fluff. From newborn through toddler, the unbleached chlorine-free diapers provide stellar absorbency and cloth-like comfort without the chemicals used in conventional brands. Get great diaper deals on Amazon.com, where a case of 136 Seventh Generation diapers sells for $42.99, making them price competitive with Pampers. You can also pick up a case of Seventh Generation Baby Wipes, also made from wood pulp fluff and moistened with aloe vera, vitamin E, and water to naturally cleanse and moisturize. A 40-pack sells for $2.99.

For an affordable biodegradable diaper, try Tushies. The gel-free, chlorine-free, and just about every other chemical-free diapers are made from cotton blended with wood pulp that is sourced from family-owned, renewable forests in Scandinavia. The diapers will biodegrade in a residential or commercial composter within 50 to 150 days. A case of 4 packs (160 diapers) is available on Amazon.com for $43.63. An 80-pack of wipes sells for 3.49.

Cloth diapers are a wise environmental choice, but sometimes an unrealistic option for those who are equal parts lazy and environmentalist. All that washing is a chore, but opting for a commercial diaper service means paying for diapers that will be washed in nasty chemicals. Plus, it's still unclear if the washing and drying of cloth diapers creates a bigger environmental impact (think of the energy output of the average washer/dryer) than the landfilling of disposable diapers. Until a clear verdict is in, we can stay a bit lazy and still make better choices for our babies and for the planet by turning to brands like Seventh Generation and Tushies. Or toilet train early. Very early.

ZWAGGLE: WHEN ALL ELSE FAILS

Even the savviest Lazy Environmentalist on a budget will eventually discover that raising a kid is an expensive endeavor. One way to circumnavigate the cost is to join Zwaggle.com, a nationwide community of parents who swap gently used baby and children's items. Joining the site is free and upon doing so you'll receive 50 Zoints (the Zwaggle currency) to get you started. The more products you pass along, the more Zoints you'll receive. You can browse items at your convenience or create a wish list—you'll be notified when your items become available. And no need to swap only with folks close to home. Products can easily be shipped using Zwaggle's integrated FedEx tool. Whether you need a stroller, baby furniture, or toys, Zwaggle can hook you up for barely a penny—you pay nothing more than shipping fees. Your kids will thank you and the environment will too—all this swapping keeps functional products out of the landfill and reduces the amount of new resources that your family consumes.

Clothing and Gear

CHAPTER ONE ORGANICS

Chapteroneorganics.com

Chapter One specializes in modern baby clothing made from 100 percent organic cotton and low-impact dyes. The striking retro patterns on the Groovy Pink and Groovy Green dresses ($38) and the Alphabet Soup onesie ($26) are the height of baby chic. The prices may be steeper than other organic options, but each piece is intentionally roomy for a longer lasting fit.

ELLAROO

Ellaroo.com

Designed for the modern parent, Ellaroo's thoughtfully designed baby carriers combine high-quality, eco-friendly materials with supreme style and comfort. The Met Hip Baby Carrier ($89) features a shoulder strap that cups the shoulder for firm support instead of riding up toward the neck. A waist strap adds additional support. It's made of organic cotton with recycled polyester batting and is available at retailers across the United States, including Babies "R" Us.

GREEN BABIES

Geenbabies.com

Founder Lynda Fassa created her organic baby clothing in 1993. Since then, Green Babies has developed into one of the most well-respected eco-baby brands available. Check out the Monkies Ls Snappy ($16) for an organic cotton rib-knit long-sleeve onesie with an adorable monkey-print design. The Cranberry Tapestry Bootleg Romper ($36) is about the cutest garment you'll find for dressing your baby girl. Each season, the line includes more than 100 different styles. You can purchase products online or use the website's store locator to find stores near you that carry Green Babies.

FOCOLOCO

Focoloco.com

Focoloco offers cool gear for cool kids. Check out the "I'm with the band" organic cotton onesie ($20). That and other hip designs are available in sizes for babies and kids up to six years old. The "Nobody Hearts Oatmeal" T-shirt ($20) made of organic cotton is an instant classic.

KATE QUINN ORGANICS

Katequinnorganics.com

Kate Quinn offers superbly styled organic cotton clothing for youngsters. Basics from onesies to collared shirts range from $16 to $28. Organic cotton dresses ($38) are playful and so exquisitely detailed that your daughter will look as though she's just stepped out of an Impressionist painting.

LOTUS PAD
Lotuspadyogamats.com
Lotus Pad knows that practicing yoga regularly helps kids perform better in school and sleep better at night and can also help reduce symptoms of ADHD. With these goals in mind, the company has created a children's line of biodegradable, PVC-free, healthy yoga mats ($28), yoga DVDs ($15), and yoga games ($19).

POSITIVELY ORGANIC
Positively-organic.com
Fair-trade, super-soft, 100 percent organic cotton is the cornerstone of Positively Organics' stylish baby clothing collection. The line is distinguished by bold, bright colors and contemporary designs. Check out the Happy Tushie Yoga Pants ($24) with a beetle, butterfly, seahorse, or flower graphic on the leg. The matching Happy Print Short Sleeve Bodysuit ($24) is all the rage in red, yellow, orange, or olive. Purchase the two together for $40.

SCKOON
Sckoon.com
Sckoon offers designer organic cotton baby clothing, cloth diapers, plush toys, and natural baby gifts. The company even makes affordable, stylish dog garments like the Organic Cotton Dog Kimono ($17.90), so you eco-accessorize your baby to match your poodle.

SPEESEES
Speesees.com
Speesees creates funky, eye-catching clothing and accessories using organic cotton and low-impact dyes to reduce chemical content. Look for 70s-inspired jumpsuits emblazoned with catchy imagery like dandelions, horses, and trees for $26. In cooler weather dress your tot in the Bear Jacket ($46) made of plush sherpa organic cotton with cute little bear ears sewn onto the hood.

TOBY+REI
Tobyandrei.com
Give your kids a stylish, eco-friendly head start with bamboo and organic cotton clothing and accessories from Toby + Rei. The organic cotton lunch sack ($18) with robot graphic makes toting lunch actually kind of cool. The Elephant Graphic T-shirt ($24) and onesie ($22) will have all the other kids wanting one (and their parents too).

Bedding and Mattresses

BABI ITALIA

Babiitalia.com

Babi Italia's Serta Perfect Balance Mattress ($179.99) utilizes a continuous innerspring coil system wrapped in layers of organic cotton and features a waterproof vinyl (but phthalate-free) cover. The mattress is available exclusively at Babies "R" Us.

KIDS LINE

Kidslineinc.om

For hip and affordable organic baby bedding, look no further than the Kids Line Bunny Meadows collection. Available exclusively at Babies "R" Us, it features a 6-piece crib set ($179) plus other key furnishings to round out your baby's room such as a hamper, musical mobile, and a lamp base and shade.

NATUREPEDIC

Naturepedic.com

Naturepedic is an eco-friendly organic mattress and bedding company founded by a group of parents, grandparents, and scientists. The No-Compromise Organic Cotton Classic baby mattress ($259) utilizes a continuous innerspring coil system wrapped in layers of organic cotton and has a cover made of food-grade, stain-resistant, nontoxic, and waterproof polyethylene.

TL CARE

Tlcare.com

This San Francisco–based maker of eco-baby bedding partners with many of the biggest retailers on the planet to offer its organic cotton products at unbeatable prices. Find crib sheets ($12.99) and reversible blankets ($12.98) at Babies "R" Us. And head to Wal-Mart to purchase a 4-piece crib set ($119.97) that includes a reversible comforter, bumper, fitted crib sheet, and crib skirt.

UNTIL KARA

Untilkara.com

Until Kara is the culmination of designer Michelle Savin's hunt for products that would be suitable for her chemical-sensitive baby. The Until Kara Mattress ($349) is made entirely of organic cotton and natural wool from organically raised sheep; the mattress's breathable wool core helps to regulate your baby's temperature by wicking away moisture.

BPA Free

ADIRI
Adiri.com
This line of BPA-free Natural Nurser Ultimate Baby Bottles are $12 and feature the unique "Fill, Twist, and Feed System," which allows for single-hand preparation. A unique "petal" vent helps reduce colic.

BORN FREE
Newbornfree.com
BornFree offers a quality line of BPA-free plastic bottles and glass bottles. Pick up a triple-pack of 5-ounce bottles complete with colic-alleviating venting system for $26.99. Trainer cups are $9.99.

NATURSUTTEN
Zoebonline.com
For an organic, all-natural, BPA-free pacifier, go for Natursutten Pacifiers ($7.95). The "better binkie" is made of pure natural rubber tapped directly from rubber trees. The one-piece design is extremely hygienic and softer than silicone (the most common pacifier material).

NUBY
Nuby.platformtwo.com
Nuby offers an entire line of colorful, affordable, BPA-free feeding gear including nursing bottles, sippy cups, utensils, food trays, and storage containers. Head to Babies "R" Us to pick up a 3-pack of 7-ounce Non-Drip Bottles for $7.95.

Toys

GREEN TOYS
Greentoys.com
For afternoon tea parties, turn to Green Toys. Made from recycled plastic milk jugs free from toxins like BPA and phthalates, the Green Toys Tea Set includes a teapot, sugar bowl, and creamer plus spoons, saucers, and cups for four ($25). Other Green Toys products include the Indoor Gardening Kit ($26), Sand Play Set ($18), and the Cookware & Dining Set ($35).

HAPE BAMBOO COLLECTION

Bamboo-collection.net

The first toy collection made from bamboo, the Hape collection includes the 120-piece Cantina stacking block set that retails for $18.95. Pandabo (about $12) is a stacking game in which players take turns stacking bamboo-like reeds and wood-shaped pieces on top of a panda. Colora ($20) and Trapecolo ($25) are puzzle games that develop pattern recognition and sequencing skills.

IMAGIPLAY

Imagiplay.com

ImagiPLAY's fun, brain-teasing products are superbly designed and made of eco-friendly materials like plantation-grown rubberwood. Products in the Natural Dream Puzzles collection are 3-dimensional wooden objects that children figure out how to assemble. Check out the Sports Car Puzzle ($16.99) and Train Puzzle ($19.99). Many other collections are also available.

KAPLA

Kaplatoys.com

For budding architects and builders, nontoxic Kapla Blocks open endless building possibilities. The solid pine wood blocks are made in France from sustainably managed forests. An introductory 40-piece set retails for $30. Visit Kaplatoys.com to view a picture gallery of the blocks in action.

MIYIM

Miyim.com

Organic stuffed characters ($25 to $30) from miYim are made of pure, untreated, unbleached, and unprocessed organic cotton combined with natural dyes derived from plants and minerals. Also look for miYim's baby's accessories (about $12 each), which include organic cotton blankets, rattles, and crib and stroller toys.

PLANTOYS

Plantoys.com

PlanToys also offers a series of eco-responsible wood toys such as rattles, rings, spin bells, as well as toy caterpillars, cars, teddy bears, and penguins that retail for under $15. Older children will love PlanToys's wooden play sets like the Railway, Road, Airport, Crane, Parking Garage, Pirate Ship, and Circus. As with all PlanToys, the sets are made with nontoxic vegetable dyes, and the solid wood comes from plantation-grown rubber trees that are harvested after their useful life as rubber producers has run its course.

Entertainment

GORILLA IN THE GREENHOUSE

Greengorilla.com

Gorilla in the Greenhouse is an action-packed animated web show that inspires kids to take real-world steps toward a healthier environment. The show is set in a magical greenhouse in San Francisco, featuring four kids and a gorilla who together use music and imagination to tackle environmental challenges facing their generation.

MEET THE GREENS

Meetthegreens.org

Meet The Greens is a cartoon series teaching kids about key environmental issues as told through the adventures of feisty Izz Green and her family members. Different webisodes address topics like clean air, conservation, and alternative energy in a fun and exciting way that frames the topics so that they are understandable for kids.

MUSIC FOR A GREEN PLANET

Musicforagreenplanet.com

Award-winning jazz musician Hayes Greenfield's album, *Music for a Green Planet,* is a compilation of jazz-infused songs with thoughtful messages. Tracks like, "We'll Be Part of the Solution" and "Things We Throw Away" will have your young ones be-bopping and scatting in no time.

WILLIAM THE GARBAGE TRUCK

Williamthegarbagetruck.com

William the Garbage Truck, co-written by James Martin II and his four-year-old son, James Martin III, is a kids' book exploring what happens when a garbage truck and his truck buddies go green. At first William appears as a gas guzzling, smoky garbage truck. As the story unfolds, William learns about conservation, makes alternative energy friends, learns lessons, and eventually transforms into a hybrid recycling truck.

Retailers

AMAZON GREEN

Amazon.com/green

Amazon.com is quickly becoming the shopping destination of choice for green baby products. Type "organic" into Amazon.com's search function and then click "baby" from the left-hand navigation bar to reveal hundreds of organic styles from reputable brands like Kee-Ka, Sckoon, Kate Quinn Organics, and

Pixel Organics. Sort the products by price from lowest to highest to find items that fall within your budget. You can also find good deals on eco-friendly diapers from brands such as Seventh Generation and Tushies.

BABIES "R" US

Babiesrus.com

Going green is easy and affordable now that Babies "R" Us offers the most extensive collection of natural and organic baby products available. Blankets, onesies, burp cloths, hooded towels, bibs, and kimonos are all for sale in organic cotton as well as booties, leggings, dresses, pants, tops, and hats. You'll also find a wide assortment of eco-friendly bedding, baby bottles, skincare, and baby gear.

FAT BRAIN TOYS

Fatbraintoys.com

Fat Brain Toys offers one of the widest selections of eco-friendly toys available, numbering well over 200 products. Click on "Green & Organic Toys" in the left-hand column to view the entire selection. Affordable finds start with a set of Smencils ($6.95), nontoxic, smelly pencils that are made from recycled newspaper. Your children's drawings will smell fruity-licious.

ECONSCIOUS MARKET

Econsciousmarket.com

A retailer with a mega-conscience, eConscious Market donates 50 percent of its profits to charity. It's easy to help the company's cause because the baby products featured are from cutting-edge green brands such as Chapter One Organics, Speesees, Jonano, Baby Greens, Cotton2U, Baby Greens, Nui Organics, Sckoon, and many more.

LOLA BABIEZ

Lolababiez.com

Lola Babiez offers 100 percent organic cotton bedding and clothing for babies and children up to four years old. The Wave Tee ($26) has snaps at the neck, to let your baby exit gracefully, and an inspired surfs-up graphic on the front. You'll also find items like the organic cotton Cuddly Bear ($12), a truly affordable eco-teddy.

WAL-MART

Walmart.com

Wal-Mart sells some of the most budget-friendly organic cotton baby goods in the world. Its exclusive George Baby line features a variety of newborn sets. A George Baby organic cotton bodysuit and reversible bib are $7. A three-piece set featuring an organic cotton bodysuit, matching shorts, and reversible bib retails for $5.92. Or pick up a set of three organic cotton body-suits for $7.88. You'll also find other eco-baby collections at Wal-Mart's unbeatable prices.

WILD DILL
Wilddill.com
Wild Dill is an eco-baby boutique that features a unique collection of contemporary products made of organic, fair-trade, sweatshop-free, natural, and sometimes even recycled materials. The Bamboo Baby Boy Jeans ($22) will be an instant hit, as will the Imagine Box Cottage ($20), a cardboard house that comes with its own set of eight nontoxic, washable watercolors. It's made of 45 percent recycled content and is 100 percent recyclable.

Information/Education

GREAT GREEN BABY
Greatgreenbaby.com
Stay on top of the latest trends in eco-baby wear and gear at this regularly updated blog. It's a terrific product resource for new and expecting parents and provides links to online stores where you can purchase the goods.

GREEN MOM FINDS
Greenmomfinds.com
Green Mom Finds provides readers with interesting articles, ways to take action on children's health and environmental standards, and links to sites with green and responsible baby products. The site is a reliable destination for learning more about child-related environmental issues.

HAUTE NATURE
Hautenature.blogspot.com
A blog tracking the latest products and trends in art and green design, Haute Nature dishes up sweet finds in the eco-kids category. Learn about a designer who makes eco-friendly stuffed animals out of repurposed wool sweaters or an artist who uses deflated balloons to make colorful wall mountings for baby rooms. You'll find something to ignite your eco-parenting imagination.

KIWI MAGAZINE
Kiwimagonline.com
Kiwi is the magazine for modern parents who want to grow their families the natural and organic way. The magazine is published bi-monthly and features excellent articles on topics like packing an organic school lunch, creating

eco-friendly craft projects, and practicing prenatal fitness techniques. You'll find lots of great content on the website too.

THE LAZY ENVIRONMENTALIST
Lazyenvironmentalist.com/kids
I've created a special page to keep Lazy Environmentalist readers updated about ongoing developments in healthy, green choices for babies and kids. Discover safe, planet-friendly and budget-friendly products and services for little ones.

MINDFUL MOMMA
Mindfulmomma.typepad.com
Mindful Momma features tips on sustainable gardening, healthy organic recipes, eco-education, and even political musings. You'll find some very creative ideas for DIY projects that you can do with your children, and the site also features links to other conscious parenting websites to help moms and dads learn more about parenting mindfully.

SWAP BABY GOODS
Swapbabygoods.com
Swap, buy, or sell baby goods at this site that recognizes how quickly babies outgrow their gear and make even the cutest onesie or sleep sack obsolete. Keep your expenses to a minimum while obtaining the baby gear you need by swapping. A zip code search box lets you quickly narrow your search to merchandise and participating parents in your area, which may be helpful when looking for bigger items like cribs, high chairs, and rocking horses.

TEENSY GREEN
Teensygreen.com
Teensy Green is a fun, informative blog written by a mom who respects those hard-core, crunchy environmentalists, but can't quite bring herself to become one. Instead, she shares insights and information about green toys, books, clothing, bath and body products, and arts and crafts. Links are provided to many other wonderful "green mom" blogs, making this site a great starting point for learning about your green child-rearing options.

ZWAGGLE
Zwaggle.com
Swap gently used baby and children's items like strollers, baby furniture, or toys with parents throughout the United States by joining Zwaggle.com. Sign up to get your Zwaggle Points (or Zoints) and use them to trade your items for the baby gear you need. The service is free aside from shipping costs, and shipping is made easy through Zwaggle's integrated FedEx tool.

10

More than Skin Deep

Earth-Friendly (Human-Safe) Personal Care Products

Today, it's easier than ever to find personal care products that help us look great without compromising our health or damaging the earth. Toothpaste, deodorant, shampoo, and soap (not to mention hair styling aids, cosmetics, and perfumes) are an everyday part of our lives, so it makes sense to choose products that are free from the toxic, petroleum-derived chemicals found in most conventional items. Selecting products that are truly safe sometimes requires us to become our own detectives, sleuthing out the origins of the product ingredients—what's *iodopropynyl butylcarbamate* anyway?—that we apply to our hair and skin. But choosing products that are truly natural or organic—and don't just claim to be—is pretty simple and increasingly affordable.

As Lazy Environmentalists, we want to make the healthiest choices for our families and ourselves while ensuring that the ingredients that go down our drains (and *all* beauty products wind up down the drain) and into our earth and water supply are as safe as can be. But since we don't have the assistance of a personal scientist to help us decipher the ingredient jargon found on most packaging, many natural personal care companies are banding together to create an industry-wide seal of approval that will simplify the process. One quick rule of thumb when shopping for natural and/or organic personal care products: Choose items made with ingredients that you can recognize. Next time you're in the shampoo aisle of your local drug store, turn around the average bottle and see how many ingredients are familiar—and pronounceable!

One company that has nothing to hide when it comes to product labeling and ingredient lists is Burt's Bees. Beginning as a homegrown beeswax candle maker in 1984, Burt's Bees gained a cultish consumer loyalty by the early 1990s with the introduction of its beeswax lip balms. Today, the company has blossomed into one of the leading natural personal care products companies in the universe with a diverse line of soaps, shampoos, moisturizers, and cosmetics. Burt's is everything you'd hope for in personal care. The products are derived from natural ingredients (like sunflower seed oil, beeswax, and rosemary leaf oil); affordable ($9.00 for 8 ounces of Carrot Nutritive Body Lotion); widely available at health food stores and major chains (like CVS, Walgreens, and Target); and, best of all, they really work. Old Burt recognized that beeswax possesses amazing capacities to naturally cleanse and moisturize the skin, and the company has gone on to integrate the healing wax into full lines of products for men, women, and babies. Check out Burt's Green Tea & Lemongrass Hand Soap, which uses coconut and sunflower oils to cleanse, green tea to soothe, and lemongrass oil to neutralize odors ($7 for a 7.5-ounce bottle). Or treat your tresses to More Moisture Raspberry and Brazil Nut Shampoo, with scalp-tingling lather and serious moisturizing—thanks to the combination of raspberry extract, honey, and Brazil nut oil ($8 for a 12-ounce bottle). Burt's also understands that women aren't the only ones who want to groom naturally. Men can beat five o'clock shadow with Natural Skin Care for Men Shave Cream, which uses calendula and chamomile to reduce inflammation and linden extract to hydrate and moisturize ($8 for a 6-ounce tube).

Burt's Bees is also at the forefront of a movement within the natural personal care industry to create standards for what constitutes a natural product. Unlike the organic food industry, personal care companies are legally permitted to label products as "natural" and "organic" even when the claims are at best half-truths and at worst entirely misleading. To rectify the situation, Burt's Bees has partnered with other leading natural personal care product companies (Aubrey Organics, Badger Balm, California Baby, Farmaesthetics, Trilogy Fragrances, and Weleda are among the participants) and the Natural Products Association (NPA) to introduce the Natural Standard and Seal. Products carrying the label have been certified by the NPA to contain at least 95 percent natural ingredients. This standard helps Lazy Environmentalists cut through the masses of health and environmental claims to quickly identify products that are as safe and natural as they claim to be. The organization has also created a list of banned substances that includes such environmental no-nos as parabens, phthalates, mineral oil, oxybenzone, and paraffin.

Recognizing a similar customer need, Whole Foods, the world's largest retailer of natural and organic products, has introduced its own Premium Body Care standard and seal of approval, intended to help its customers quickly identify high-quality, natural products. Customers shopping in the Whole Body section of Whole Foods can select products that carry the seal to ensure that the products they're purchasing are top-rated for safety, quality, and environmental impact.

Another leader in the push for a greener personal care industry is Teens Turning Green. The innovative organization harnesses the creativity, determination, and tenacity of teenagers who want to live in a country where safe personal care products are the norm. The coalition of young women aims to educate the public about the use of harmful ingredients in cosmetics and other grooming products. So far, the teens have successfully lobbied for political legislation in California (in 2005 they helped to pass SB484, the California Safe Cosmetics Act); engaged major corporations in constructive dialogue, and are working with Whole Foods to create a collective brand of natural products under the label "Teens Turning Green." If you're a teenager ready to engage in positive environmental change (or a parent or adult who's interested in the cause), check out Teensforsafecosmetics.org to see how you can participate.

The market trends outlined here make it simple for Lazy Environmentalists to identify healthy, eco-aware products today. Yet, the ultimate value of these safe items is the impact they'll have on tomorrow. Certifications and seals of approval help to create a circle of positive change. As it becomes easier for consumers to identify (and afford) legitimate natural products, we'll select these brands more often. And the more natural and organic products we purchase, the more profitable these companies become, which in

Judy Shills is the founder of Teens Turning Green, an organization led by teens that raises awareness about potentially harmful ingredients in beauty and daily use products.

How did you get the idea for Teens Turning Green?
Back when my daughter was about 12 and I was leading an effort to discover why Marin County, California, had high rates of cancer, I wanted to engage the passion and wisdom of young people in an issue that would have direct impact on their lives. I figured that if I told my daughter not to use a product that I thought was potentially toxic even though quite popular, she might just borrow it from a friend. But if she and other young women became educated about the potential health risks of the products they were using on their bodies, they might just decide to make changes in their own lives. So in 2005, we set out with a group of teens to change their world and ultimately generations to come.

What is Teens Turning Green's positive environmental impact?
When you engage young women (sometimes young men join us too) in an initiative that affects their health and well being, you see the best of their ability. As our base of teens grows, so does the opportunity to have a large impact. The choices teens collectively make can force change in the way companies do business. For example, one of the companies who wanted to be in our new "Teens Turning Green" line completely reformulated its mask to eliminate chemicals and comply with our standards.

Another big piece of our work is advocacy. Our teens have lobbied successfully in the state of California to affect legislation. In October 2005, the first Safe Cosmetics Act was signed into law by Governor Schwarzenegger as a result of their 11th-hour lobbying. They had a hand in the Toxic Toys Bill passage in 2007, and in June 2008, they headed to Sacramento to lobby for a bill that would ban lead in lipstick and for another that would ban Bisphenol-A in children's toys.

Can teenagers really make a difference?
Absolutely and in profound ways. People are routinely mesmerized by the ability of our teen campaign members to articulate and engage others around this core issue, whether through a high school assembly or a visit to the state capitol. Teachers, parents, business leaders, and politicians want to learn from them and work with them. Teens are a very powerful and empowered demographic. Once they get educated on the issues, they educate all who will listen. They make the biggest difference.

turn tells the manufacturers of conventional products that they need to change the ingredients of their own goods to qualify for the certifications and seals of approval that consumers look for when selecting products. Clear labels, legitimate seals of approval, and third-party verifications are the fastest way to transform the entire personal care industry so that one day every product we put on our bodies will truly be safe and effective.

Personal Care Brands

ALBA
Albaorganics.com
Alba is quickly gaining recognition and shelf space for its affordable, lightly scented products made from herbal extracts, botanical oils, and plant pro-teins. In addition to fruit-based facial scrubs, cleaners, and body products ($8.95 to $11.95) that naturally restore antioxidants to enhance skin tone and luster, the company's patented green tea shampoos and conditioners help restore natural and color-treated hair without using harmful ingredi-ents.

AVALON ORGANICS
Avalonorganics.com
This chemical-free skin care and hair care line offers both lipid-rich fragrant products as well as fragrant-free products sourced in northern California's Sonoma region. Products range from a natural anti-aging rinse ($11.95), made from fermented vegetables, to a wrinkle prevention serum ($24.95)

made from jojoba and sunflower oil, to mild baby soaps and shampoos ($9.95) made from chamomile and aloe. The company's earth-friendly commitment extends to its warehouse and offices that are 100 percent solar-powered.

BURT'S BEES

Burtsbees.com

Burt's is everything you'd hope for in a personal care company. The products are derived from natural ingredients like sunflower seed oil, beeswax, and rosemary leaf oil. They're affordable ($9.00 for 8 ounces of Carrot Nutritive Body Lotion), widely available, and best of all, they really work. Old Burt recognized that beeswax possesses amazing capacities to naturally cleanse and moisturize the skin, and the company has gone on to integrate the healing wax into full lines of products for men, women, and babies.

CLEAN WELL

Cleanwelltoday.com

This patented, all-natural hand sanitizer is 100 percent chemical-free, biodegradable, and daresay a revolutionary step forward in green beauty technology. Cleanwell kills 99.9 percent of all germs, including *E. coli*, staph, salmonella, and cooties, but without the use of hazardous chemicals found in standard hand sanitizers. Instead, Cleanwell uses a new natural compound called Ingenium which is both easier to pronounce and much less hazardous for your family. Purchase a 6-pack for $16.99.

GIOVANNI

Giovannicosmetics.com

Giovanni shampoos, conditioners, and serums (around $7.99 each) trick your mind (and your hair) into thinking that you've just purchased a very exclusive and expensive salon-only product, when in reality you've bought an organic, effective, and widely available alternative for just a fraction of the price.

KISS MY FACE

Kissmyface.com

For more than 20 years, Kiss My Face has been "obsessively natural" about the ingredients used in its soaps, shampoos, conditioners, cleansers, lotions, sunscreens, makeup, deodorants, toothpastes, and lip balms (find them for under $9.99 each). The cornerstone of its products is antioxidant-rich olive oil, which naturally reduces redness, tightens skin, and stimulates new cell generation.

JASON

Jasoncosmetics.com

A natural cosmetic company that meets many beauty product needs in addition to soap and shampoo, JASON's extensive line also includes organic, all-natural alternatives to conventional arthritis relief lotion, anti-aging serum, and even skin bleaching cream. Products typically range from $5 to $25.

JUICE BEAUTY

Juicebeauty.com

Juice Beauty uses freshly squeezed organic juice concentrate as the foundation for its natural beauty products. In addition to juice, products are formulated using pure and organic ingredients such as aloe vera, honey, botanicals, plant oils, and raw cane sugar. A men's organic line is also available. Most Juice Beauty products range between $19.99 and $49.99.

PACIFIC SHAVING OIL

Pacificshaving.com

Forget about bothering with shaving cream when just seven drops of Pacific Shaving Oil's natural solution will give you the closest shave of your life. A half-ounce bottle ($6.95) provides up to 100 shaves. This miracle product relies upon essential oils to perform its magic. The tiny bottle is great for air travel too, since you can stow it conveniently in a carry-on bag.

PANGEA

Pangeaorganics.com

From its organic products ingredients grown on wind-powered, fair wage, collectively owned, all-female farms in Africa, to the biodegradable packaging with embedded flower seeds that sprout once you've buried them in the backyard, Pangea is an all around eco-dynamo. It's also one of the fastest growing companies in the natural personal care category, thanks to products that are exceptionally formulated. Try the Pangea Organic Indian Lemongrass & Rosemary Shower Gel ($14) for a vibrant, sensuous experience that will jump-start your morning.

WELEDA

Weleda.com

Weleda has been formulating high-quality natural cosmetics for more than 85 years. From sensitive skin cleansers ($9.99) that use sweet almond oil, plum kernel oil, and blackthorn blossoms to a lemon-based body wash ($14.99) that replenishes skin by increasing its collagen and elastin, Weleda naturally knows its stuff and draws upon years of experience to provide affordable natural products that really work.

Online Retailers

AMAZON.COM

Online powerhouse Amazon.com is great for CDs and books and also offers one of the most extensive inventories of sustainable beauty products available. To shop for products from more than 50 green beauty brands, just enter "organic" in the search box on the Amazon.com home page and follow the "personal care" link to see all of the goods.

FUTURE NATURAL

Futurenatural.com

Future Natural offers organic products that range from high-end luxury to super-affordable in areas of skin care, hair care, nail care, makeup, and fragrance. The shopper-friendly website is easy to use and offers product reviews for hard-to-find and interesting beauty products. For example, the Juniper Ridge Wild Herb Soap Slab ($6.50) in Coastal Sage is made of a vegetable base and shea butter and, according to Future Natural, "distinctly smells of California's central to southern coast."

COSMETICS KITCHEN

Cosmeticskitchen.com

Cosmetics Kitchen features off-the-beaten-path beauty products for all types of consumers—moms, dads, teens, mommies-to-be, etc. The natural cosmetics, mineral makeup, body and skin care, and bath products are uniquely crafted to accommodate different skin types and help you put your best face forward.

TARGET

Target.com

Target is expanding its beauty product selection to include a stellar selection of organic beauty products. Hundreds of natural products are available, including products from many of the leading brands featured in this chapter's resource list.

WHITE RABBIT BEAUTY

Whiterabbitbeauty.com

A one-stop shop for sustainable beauty products that are high quality and cruelty free, White Rabbit Beauty carries cleansing products, nail polish, fragrances, and makeup with an emphasis on humane treatment of animals. Makeup fans will be delighted with the vast array of plant-based foundations, vitamin C–rich mascaras, and extensive fragrance-free body and hair products.

Ones to Watch

PRITI ORGANICS
Pritiorganicspa.com
Relax at this organic day spa in New York City. Priti also retails its own line of nontoxic nail lacquers that come in bright, rich colors. Most nail polishes are paint-based, but Priti formulates its own using natural soy-based dyes. You can purchase the products online by visiting the company's website.

NATURAL PRODUCTS ASSOCIATION
Naturalproductsassoc.org
In 2008, the Natural Products Association (NPA) introduced the Natural Standard and Seal, a product certification that verifies that products are made of at least 95 percent natural ingredients. This standard helps Lazy Environmentalists cut through the masses of health and environmental claims to quickly identify products that are as safe and natural as they claim to be.

PHYSICIANS FORMULA ORGANIC
Organicwearmakeup.com
Physicians Formula is a well-known cosmetics company that is actively moving into the realm of thoughtful, organic beauty. Through the introduction of its new Organic Wear line of products—made without harsh dyes, chemicals, or toxic ingredients—the company is helping to make green grooming options available to a wider audience.

TEENS TURNING GREEN
Teensturninggreen.org
This teen-led organization raises awareness about potentially harmful ingredients in beauty and daily use products. Teens have successfully lobbied for political legislation in California, engaged major corporations in constructive dialogue, and are working with Whole Foods to create a collective brand of natural products under the label "Teens Turning Green."

Information/Education

BEAUTIFUL REVIEW
Beautifulreview.com
Search the largest and most up-to-date database of third-party beauty product reviews. The quick search drop-down menu lets you review products by brand. Natural and organic skin care products are reviewed along with conventional products.

SKIN DEEP

Cosmeticsdatabase.com

The Skin Deep database analyzes more than 25,000 cosmetics products to check for ingredients that are hazardous to human health. You can review specific products and brands to see how safe they really are for your body. It's an excellent tool for quickly making informed purchasing decisions for you and your family.

ECO-LABELS

Greenerchoices.org / eco-labels

With so many competing claims on what constitutes an environmentally sound product, this website from Consumer Reports helps you cut through the confusion. The site explains different eco-labels and lets you know which are substantive and which are bogus. Learn about personal care products and also research other product categories such as food and household cleaners.

THE GREEN MAKEUP ARTIST

Greenmakeupartist.com

Bridal parties can sign up to have an experienced cosmetics professional prep everyone—the bride, mother of the bride, and bridesmaids—using organic products and techniques. Check the website's blog for insider tips on looking fabulous naturally.

THE LAZY ENVIRONMENTALIST

Lazyenvironmentalist.com / skin

I've created a special page to keep Lazy Environmentalist readers updated about ongoing developments in natural and organic personal care products. Stay on top of affordable solutions for looking your best on the outside while feeling your best on the inside.

11

Create an
Eco-Office

A few years ago, going green in the office was often
viewed as nothing more than a distraction from day-to-day business. Today, interoffice eco-initiatives are seen as invaluable tools for generating cost-savings, boosting company morale, and attracting younger, eco-conscious talent. To create an eco-friendly working environment it's essential to consider the way your company uses energy, the type of supplies that find their way into the supply closet, and how employees commute to the workplace. But greening the office need not be a chore. New eco-advanced solutions can make the job easy, fun, and cost-effective. However, to get those solutions to stick it's essential to engage employees and show how green initiatives are good for the corporate bottom line as well as employees' bottom line. Here's how.

USE ECO-OFFICE SUPPLIES
Major retailers are lining up to help you easily green the contents of your supply closet. Staples leads the charge with its EcoEasy program available at Staples.com/ecoeasy. The shopping site offers more than 2,200 office products made using recycled content. Whether you're on the hunt for desktop organizers, bulletin boards, binders, folders, notepads, sticky notes, or scissors, Staples has the supplies to boost productivity while reducing your eco-impact. Recycled ink and toner cartridges are available at discounted prices, and Staples will even reward you for considering the planet: Bring back your empty ink or toner cartridges for recycling, and Staples will give you a $3 in-store credit for each one.

The office is also an effective place to tap your inner treehugger. That's because the average employee consumes an entire tree's worth of paper every year. Conservation is really about the choices we make while sitting at our desks. Political and organizational affiliations aside, everybody loves trees. Well, everyone who enjoys breathing oxygen that is (where did you think oxygen came from? Scuba tanks? Oprah?). About 50 percent of the world's oxygen supply comes from trees and other plants—the rest comes from blue-green algae and plankton in the ocean. Stocking your office with recycled paper products not only helps you and everyone else breathe easier, but it also helps prevent greenhouse gas emissions. According to the United Nations, today global deforestation generates 25 to 30 percent of all greenhouse gas emissions. That's because growing trees feed on carbon dioxide and mature trees store it in their extensive root systems. Doing our part to keep trees healthy and thriving is good for forests and for us.

Staples, Office Depot, and OfficeMax make doing our part for the forests easy. One hundred percent recycled office paper — copier, multiuse, as well as more specialized varieties for inkjet and laser printing—is widely available and competitively priced. Switching to recycled paper also saves about half the energy and water needed to make paper in the first place. If going the recycled route isn't an option, your next best bet is to look for paper that carries the FSC (Forest Stewardship Council) label, certifying that the wood used in the paper-making process originated from a responsibly managed forest.

GET NEWS DIGITALLY

Reduce paper consumption further by tapping into digital media. Newspapers and magazines are easier than ever to read on computers and other digital devices. *The New York Times* and *Washington Post* offer free online access to registered readers, as do many regional newspapers. And *The Wall Street Journal* offers a digital subscription for $79 per year (the same rate as the print edition).

If scanning magazines is the way you stay on top of business trends, check out the digital subscriptions available through Zinio. com. More than 500 major magazines like *Business Week*, *Advertising Age*, *Cosmopolitan*, *Car & Driver*, *Men's Health*, *Dwell*, *Outside*, and *Yoga Journal* are available. Download the Zinio Reader and read the magazines on your computer or access your subscriptions online from any computer at Zinio.com. iPhone owners can even access full magazines through their phones. Digital subscriptions cut costs too. For example, a digital subscription to *Cosmopolitan* costs $12 on Bn.com—Barnes & Noble teamed up with Zinio in 2008 to offer the service on its own site—compared to $18 for the print subscription. Zinio lets you purchase individual issues too. No need to dispatch the office intern to the newsstand. Magazine reading is now both green *and* lazy—just the way we like it.

GREEN THE OFFICE EQUIPMENT

Doing your job efficiently often demands quick access to numerous electronic products. The efficient way to choose energy-efficient office equipment—computers, copiers, printers, and fax machines—is to look for the Energy Star label when purchasing. A jointly administered program of the EPA and the U.S. Department of Energy, Energy Star–qualified electronics can use up to 60 percent less energy than conventional products. Visit Energystar.gov for a list of products that make the cut. And check out the "Special Offers" link, which features a searchable database of local rebates, credits, and sales tax exemptions for Energy Star products.

You can search for the greenest computers available at Epeat. net, the online home of the Electronic Product Environmental Assessment Tool, a program from the Green Electronics Council. Products are evaluated based on lengthy criteria, including energy efficiency, toxicity of materials, recycled and renewable material content, ease of recyclability, product life expectancy, and overall eco-responsibility of the manufacturer. Toshiba's models currently dominate the laptop category, Dell rules the desktop arena, and Lenovo takes the gold in monitors. But the race is tight, and others like HP and Apple are quickly gaining ground.

Before purchasing a new Energy Star– or EPEAT-certified product, be sure to visit RefurbDepot.com, where the inventory is deep and the deals are huge. As the name suggests, RefurbDepot.com sells refurbished desktops and laptop computers, printers, scanners, copy machines, fax machines, and much more. Refurbished items are typically products that were returned within 30 days of purchase, had damaged packaging or a slight cosmetic defect, were used as in-store display items, or were simply overstocked. Products are fixed, repackaged, and frequently sold for more than 50 percent off the retail price. Many are still covered by their original warranties. For refurbished Blackberries, iPods, and other cell phones and MP3 players, visit Dyscern.com. Dell devotees can check out Delloutlet.com for a selection of the brand's own refurbished items. Taking advantage of these bargains helps keep these products out of landfills, which is where they would otherwise end up.

INSTALL ENERGY CONTROLS

We're taught as children to turn off lights when leaving a room, but the lesson can fade as we become adults. We forget or get distracted. Sometimes we're lazy or too tired. And at the office we may pass it off as someone else's responsibility. Instead of pinning blame on your co-workers for leaving the bathroom, supply closet, or conference room lights on, get a little automated help. Occupancy sensors are designed to automatically turn lights on when rooms are occupied and off when empty. Watt Stopper's occupancy sensors cost less than $40 and fit into regular light switch wall plates. You can still turn lights on or off manually or let the Watt Stopper do it for you.

Workers can also benefit from the Watt Stopper Isolé IDP-3050, an 8-outlet power strip equipped with an occupancy sensor to automatically shut off items when not in use ($90). Two of the outlets are controlled manually (sensor-free) to give users the flexibility to keep electronics like hard drives and fax machines running even when workstations are vacated. Visit Chooserenewables.com for a wide selection of Watt Stopper products. Belkin offers a similar 8-outlet power strip ($49.99), which, while lacking an occupancy sensor, comes with a remote control device to shut down electronics completely without reaching behind your desk to unplug them—electronics use energy even when shut off (see Chapter 4: Energy for more information about this "vampire effect").

Jerry Mix is co-founder and president of Watt Stopper, a company that makes energy-efficient devices to stop energy waste.

How did you get the idea for Watt Stopper?
There were several factors that led to my wanting to create sensors that saved energy. My father was an early environmentalist and created the first phosphate-free laundry detergent. Also, living through the gas crisis of the 1970s, conservation became an important issue for us. In the early '80s, I read a book about conservation and the environment and saw opportunity. The focus on lighting controls came when we'd drive through the streets of San Francisco at night and see just about every building with all the lights on, wasting enormous amounts of energy.

What is Watt Stopper's positive environmental impact?
Every product that Watt Stopper makes has the goal of stopping energy waste in buildings or homes. It's great knowing that each time we send out products, they will work to cut energy usage, whether it's in a large high-rise or your kid's bedroom. Lately, we've been working on making our products comply with stringent environmental codes, such as Europe's RoHS, which reduces the amount of metal and hazardous material and makes the products more recyclable.

Would you say this is an accurate statement: "Stop the watts now and nobody gets hurt"?
We have nothing against watts, they are useful to us in so many ways. But overindulging in watts is where we can definitely get into trouble. The problems we're facing with the environment are too big for just a few to solve. Everyone must get involved to help so no one does get hurt. So for us, it comes down to stopping as many watts as possible. For every watt stopped, we can eliminate three watts from production.

IMPROVE THE COMMUTE

When it comes to commuting, the most environmentally unfriendly—and lonely—way to travel is by yourself in your own car. While you're stuck in traffic, inhaling noxious fumes, and staring at the bumper stickers on the car in front of you, life is passing you by in the HOV (High Occupancy Vehicle) lane. Luckily, there are many wallet- and mental health–friendly alternatives to your solo ride. Buses and commuter trains in cities around the country are beginning to offer free, Wi-Fi Internet access. Services like Nuride.com and Zimride.com are making carpooling easier and more fun than ever before. And vanpooling is giving new life to the multipassenger vehicle (see Chapter 3: Tread Lightly for a full discussion of commuting options).

ELIMINATE THE COMMUTE

Young, ambitious, investment bankers and corporate lawyers know that you can eliminate the commute by spending bleary-eyed nights cramped on the office couch. For the rest of us, living in the office only makes sense if our office is in our home. Welcome to the world of telecommuting, where pajama day is every day— as long as you don't have a videoconference scheduled with your boss. Citrix offers a suite of handy telecommuting tools to boost your at-home productivity including GoToMyPC, a fast, easy, and secure way to remotely access your office computer from any other Internet-connected computer. Whether you're at your kitchen table, in a coffee shop, or on the beach, the software allows you to operate the computer you use at work exactly as if you were sitting in your cubicle. For $19.95 per month, you can access files, read and respond to email messages, and print documents. And so you don't miss out on the weekly meeting, GoToMeeting lets you host or join meetings online and even do sales presentations using your PowerPoint slides. For $39 per month with an annual plan, GoToMeeting also lets you conduct training sessions and give product demonstrations. So go ahead and take care of business while chilling on the patio. No commute means no car-related expenses or greenhouse gas emissions. What's not to like?

CREATE BUY-IN

As much as we might cajole, beg, and dare them, co-workers and employees rarely adopt long-term green behavior just because "it's the right thing to do." To make green initiatives stick, you've got to prove that reducing, reusing, and recycling is mutually beneficial (for the planet and for employees). But changing any aspect of a company's culture rarely happens overnight, and shifting the culture toward greater eco-responsibility is no exception. Remember, reaching eco-office nirvana is about both the journey and the destination. There are four key components to creating an effective and long-lasting corporate eco-culture: 1) announce what you propose to change; 2) state your expectations of participation; 3) measure and share results; 4) reward when targets are met. Do this and you'll meet less resistance (or you'll at least whittle it away over time). Here's how you might approach an initiative to "reduce paper."

» Announce your intention to reduce paper use by 25 percent over the next two months.

» State that everyone is expected to participate by printing less.

» Adjust the default setting on all office printers to double-sided printing. Office workers will be reminded every time they click print that environmental change is under way.

» Measure how much paper is used each month, and report the numbers to everyone (measuring directly connects employee actions to results and demonstrates that your company takes its green initiatives seriously).

» When the target is reached, reward with something fun. It doesn't have to be big. It just has to be valued. Treat employees to fresh-baked organic cupcakes; throw an organic martini happy hour; or sponsor a company outing to a farmers' market. By celebrating the company's eco-success, you'll encourage more eco-victories.

Office Products and Services

BELKIN CONSERVE SURGE PROTECTOR
Belkin.com
The Belkin Conserve is eight-outlet power strip ($49.99) that comes with a remote control device to let you easily shut off electronics—and completely kill the power—without having to bend over or reach behind your desk to unplug them from the wall. Save money, save energy, and save your back.

GOTOMEETING
Gotomeeting.com
Telecommuters can remotely participate in life at the office with GoToMeeting, a software solution that lets you host or join meetings online and even do sales presentations using your PowerPoint slides. For $39 per month with an annual plan, GoToMeeting also lets you conduct training sessions and give product demonstrations.

GOTOMYPC
Gotomypc.com
A terrific tool for telecommuters, GoToMyPC is a fast, easy, and secure way to remotely access your office computer from any other Internet-connected computer. The software allows you to operate the computer you use at work exactly as if you were sitting in your cubicle. For $19.95 per month, you can access files, read and respond to email messages, and print documents.

SMART STRIP POWER STRIP
Smarthomeusa.com
Use this 10-outlet power strip (around $40) to connect the on/off status of your computer peripherals—speakers, scanner, printer, etc.—to the on/off status of your computer. This way when you turn off your computer, the Smart Strip automatically shuts off the other devices that are plugged into it. This is an easy way to save money by saving energy. And three manually controlled outlets give you flexibility to leave items like hard drives and fax machines on even when your computer is off.

WATT STOPPER
Wattstopper.com
A company with a mission to stop energy waste, Watt Stopper's occupancy motion sensors (under $40) automatically turn lights on when rooms are occupied and off when rooms are empty. The company's Isolé IDP-3050 8-outlet power strip ($90) applies the same technology to your office electronics. The power strip's internal occupancy sensor turns on computers

and other electronics when your office is occupied and off again when it's vacated. Two manually controlled outlets offer flexibility to leave items like hard drives and fax machines continually running.

ZINIO
Zinio.com

Zinio takes you into the age of digital magazines and reduces the need for all that paper. At Zinio.com, you can subscribe to more than 500 titles like *BusinessWeek, Advertising Age, Cosmopolitan, Car & Driver, Men's Health, Dwell, Outside,* and *Yoga Journal.* Download the Zinio Reader and read the magazines on your computer or access your subscriptions online from any computer at Zinio.com. iPhone owners can even access entire magazines through their phones.

Office Supply Retailers

DELL OUTLET
Delloutlet.com

Find tremendous deals on Dell products by shopping the company's inventory of refurbished items. Desktop and laptop computers, servers, monitors, and laser printers are available at up to 40 percent off retail prices. Products are sold with the same customer support, delivery options, and warranties as new items.

THE GREEN OFFICE
Thegreenoffice.com

The Green Office is an office supplies retailer dedicated exclusively to green products. To simplify the shopping experience, the company has created "green screen" icons that help you quickly ascertain whether a product is third-party certified, contains recycled content, has reduced chemical content, and/or is biodegradable or compostable.

DYSCERN
Dyscern.com

For amazing deals on refurbished iPods, Blackberries, PDAs, and other cell phones, look no further than Dyscern.com. The inventory is extensive at this online retailer that specializes in the recovery and resale of products that would otherwise end up in landfills.

OFFICE DEPOT

Officedepot.com/buygreen
In an effort to make eco-office supply shopping easier, Office Depot launched the "Your Greener Office" site in 2008. A quick visit reveals hundreds of items that will keep you working productively while reducing your eco-impact.

OFFICEMAX

Officemax.com
Visit the OfficeMax website to search for products under the header "Environmentally Preferable Products," and you'll find plenty to choose from, like steel office furniture and paper products made with recycled content. OfficeMax has also partnered with a company called TerraCycle to offer a line of affordable recycled office and school supplies that includes binders, waste baskets, pencil pouches, backpacks, lunchboxes, and homework folders.

REFURB DEPOT

Refurbdepot.com
Visit Refurbdepot.com to find tremendous deals on refurbished desktops and laptop computers, printers, scanners, copy machines, fax machines, and much more. Many items are still covered by their original warranties and frequently sold for more than 50 percent off the retail price.

STAPLES

Staples.com/ecoeasy
Staples's EcoEasy program makes it easy to identify and purchase eco-aware office products. Shop for recycled paper products, natural cleaners, and Energy Star–rated electronics with just a click of your mouse.

Information/Education

ENERGY STAR

Energystar.gov
This jointly administered program of the U.S. Department of Energy and the EPA makes purchasing energy-efficient electronics as easy as choosing products carrying the Energy Star label. Energy Star products are up to 60 percent more energy efficient than standard products and available in more than 50 categories, including computers, printers, copiers, fax machines, scanners, and even water coolers. Click on "Special Offers" to find local rebates, credits, and sales tax exemptions for Energy Star products.

EPEAT

Epeat.net

EPEAT (Electronic Product Environmental Assessment Tool) is a program from the Green Electronics Council. Search the site's database to find out which desktop and laptop computers and monitors are the most eco-responsible. Products are evaluated based on lengthy criteria, including energy efficiency, toxicity of materials, recycled and renewable material content, ease of recyclability, product life expectancy, and overall eco-responsibility of the manufacturer.

THE LAZY ENVIRONMENTALIST

Lazyenvironmentalist.com / office

I've created a special page to keep Lazy Environmentalist readers updated about easy and affordable ways to create an eco-office. Discover new products, services, and technologies that can help you maximize your productivity while minimizing your eco-impact.

12

Kick-Start
your
Environmental
Career

Green Gigs

Whether we live to work or work to live, one thing is for sure—Americans spend most of their time on the job. And though many of us would like to dedicate those working hours to a cause we can feel good about, something that would motivate us to get up every day—besides simply paying the bills—it hasn't been easy to align our philosophical leanings with employment opportunities. But times have changed. Today, it's increasingly possible to earn a good living while promoting positive environmental change. As the twenty-first century clean economy takes hold, established companies are greening their business operations in substantive ways, new green companies are forming to bring innovative environmental solutions to market, and local governments are striving to clean their cities and create healthier communities. All of this economic activity translates into more green jobs. Applying your professional know-how in the name of a cleaner planet has never been easier. Here are some Lazy Environmentalist strategies for finding the ultimate green job.

BUILD CREDENTIALS

Depending upon your industry, you can give your career a green boost and build your credentials by becoming certified in a specific green area. Those with careers tied to the building industry can become accredited by the U.S. Green Building Council, the driving force behind today's green building boom. LEED (Leadership in Environmental and Energy Design) accreditation is typically sought by real estate developers, architects, interior designers, engineers, contractors, product manufacturers and suppliers, and consultants who advise on the development of green building projects. In 2004 there were roughly 10,000 LEED-accredited professionals in the United States working on green building projects. By 2008 the number had swelled to more than 40,000 professionals.

The demand for green buildings is creating accreditation opportunities in related industries as well. EcoBroker International offers green certification for licensed real estate agents. The certification equips them with the knowledge to advise both residential and commercial clients on the environmental merits of every type of building, from houses and apartments to office parks and manufacturing facilities. More than 3,000 certified EcoBrokers are currently practicing around the country, and the numbers are rising.

DEVELOP SKILLS

Finding work in the green economy is not always as easy as simply applying for a job. Some positions require special skills sets and knowledge, and those equipped with the new know-how are often in high demand. For example, throughout Southern California, many cities are turning to alternative fuels to run their public vehicle fleets. Buses, garbage trucks, street sweepers, sewer cleaners, maintenance trucks, and other municipality-owned vehicles are increasingly being run on cleaner fuels to combat local air pollution and reduce greenhouse gas emissions. These new and improved vehicles require trained technicians to service their fleets. That's why just east of Los Angeles at the Rio Hondo College of Automotive Technology, aspiring technicians can enroll in the school's Alternative Fuel Training Program. The two-year program trains students to work on vehicles that run on cleaner power sources such as electric, hydrogen, fuel cell, compressed natural gas, liquid natural gas, biodiesel, and ethanol. Students also learn to work with hybrid engine technologies and other advanced engine systems. The program was pioneered by John Frala, professor of Automotive Technology and co-coordinator of the Alternative Fuel Program at Rio Hondo. According to Frala, program graduates are in high demand. Graduating technicians can expect to earn starting salaries between $18 and $22 per hour.

Rio Hondo is one of 29 schools around the United States that belong to the National Alternative Fuels Training Consortium

(NAFTC). Headquartered at West Virginia University, the NAFTC conducts workshops and helps coordinate and develop curriculums for its educational institution members in alternative fuels, alternative fuel vehicles, and advanced technologies. To date, more than 7,500 technicians have been trained to handle the nation's emerging fleets of alternative fuel vehicles. To find out about programs near you, visit the NAFTC's website at Naftc.wvu.edu.

Military veterans returning from active duty overseas are also entering job training programs to find work in the green economy. Integrating back into American society can prove challenging for those who were once in the armed forces. While the average U.S. unemployment rate hovers around 5 percent, for veterans the number is typically closer to 15 percent. To combat this problem, in 2007 Jyl Dehaven, a Dallas-based green building entrepreneur, started Green Collar Vets, a nonprofit organization that steers veterans toward green job opportunities. Veterans receive training in high-growth green building–related industries learning to install everything from solar panels to natural wall plasters.

Training for green jobs is also raising economic prospects for individuals on the lowest rungs of the socioeconomic ladder. One of the most powerful environmental crusades emerging today is the green collar job movement spearheaded by leaders like Van Jones of the Ella Baker Center for Human Rights in Oakland, California, and Majora Carter of Sustainable South Bronx in Bronx, New York. Their work has helped focus attention on the idea that green collar jobs can lift millions of people out of poverty by placing them in jobs that clean up communities, roll back global warming, increase our energy independence, and build a powerful economy that operates in balance with nature. Jones and Carter co-founded Green for All, an organization dedicated to building a broad coalition of support for green collar jobs. In 2007, they were instrumental in pressing Congress to pass the Green Jobs Act, which authorized $125 million per year to create a federal Energy Efficiency and Renewable Energy Worker Training Program. Green collar jobs are as diverse as the people doing them. They include retrofitting buildings for energy efficiency, installing solar panels and green roofs, building wind farms, and refining waste oil into biodiesel. In many communities across the country, training initiatives are already under way. Visit Greenforall.org to learn how the green economy is lifting people out of poverty.

TAP INTO RENEWABLE ENERGY

Green job opportunities can also be found in the creation of clean, renewable energy sources like solar and wind. And it's happening in the heart of the Rust Belt in Toledo, Ohio. Once a global leader in glass manufacturing for the automobile industry, Toledo watched its economy steadily decline as jobs were lost to lower-cost factories overseas. Today, Toledo's glass manufacturing expertise is attracting a new industry. The city is emerging as an important innovation center in the rapidly growing solar energy industry. Next-generation solar energy companies are developing low-cost ways to create solar panels by printing them on glass—a technology known as "thin film solar." As a result, more than 5,000 solar manufacturing jobs have been created in Toledo in the past few years. Research and development is playing a key role in Toledo's manufacturing renaissance, and the University of Toledo is where much of the activity is happening. The school's Thin Film Silicon Photovoltaic Laboratory is helping to develop commercial technologies that give local businesses a competitive edge. One of those businesses is Xunlight, a company that received more than $20 million in venture capital funding in 2008 and immediately began hiring engineers and technicians to work at its Toledo-based facility.

Across the border in Pennsylvania, former steel workers are using their skills to promote another clean energy industry. In 2007, Gamesa, a Spanish wind turbine manufacturer, and the United Steel Workers union concluded an agreement to open two wind turbine manufacturing facilities in the hills of western Pennsylvania. The partnership created 1,200 good paying jobs in the process. As the U.S. wind energy industry expands, international manufacturers are realizing that it's good business to be close to its customers. This thinking led Danish company Vestas, the largest wind turbine manufacturer in the world, to open its first U.S. manufacturing

Jyl Dehaven is co-founder and board president of Green Collar Vets, an organization that coordinates skill development, education, and employment opportunities in emerging green industries for U.S. military veterans.

How did you get the idea for Green Collar Vets?

I got the idea for Green Collar Vets when I was working with another nonprofit organization and started hearing about the difficulties and horror stories that young men and women were experiencing when they returned from their deployments. These people chose to serve their country and risk their lives so that I didn't have to, and then upon returning found that employment was difficult at best and impossible at worst. This just didn't work for me. Since I was already involved in the "green" industry and saw the huge employment opportunities, it seemed a natural marriage.

What is Green Collar Vets's positive environmental impact?

Green Collar Vets has had a positive environmental impact at a basic level by filling a gap in staffing. Green industries are growing by leaps and bounds, and one of the big missing pieces has always been finding quality personnel who want to "change careers" and learn a different way of doing things. Veterans have historically already learned how to pick up new skills and apply them in their job(s) during their military career. Taking the "green" skills and applying them usually comes easy to these folks.

As to environmental impact specifically, no matter your political view, I think most people will agree that we have found ourselves as a nation defending our independence based on the reality that we have become dependent on foreign fossil fuels. Whether you consider this perspective environmental or patriotic, what better group of people would you want to help take our country back to the independent powerhouse that we historically have represented? Veterans are an honorable group of people who have already proven their dedication to this country. At the very least, they deserve the opportunity to create careers that support their/our country's independence.

Objectively speaking, which is tougher; military basic training or green collar job training?
There is really no comparison between military basic training and green collar job training. No question, what our young men and women go through when they experience military basic training is probably the best and toughest training that they can have. That is yet another reason why they make such amazing employees. Military training teaches them to be warriors and to defend themselves, their team, and this nation. Green collar job training helps take some of those skills and redirects them to build strong careers and hopefully, in the long run, a stronger country.

facility in Windsor, Colorado, and Siemens, the German industrial conglomerate, to do the same in Fort Madison, Iowa. Contrary to popular belief, the green energy economy won't be powered by the corn fields of Iowa (which are used to create ethanol) but by the domestic-built wind turbines towering above them. Wind-powered turbines will also be seen towering over the Texas panhandle, where legendary oil man T. Boone Pickens is building the world's largest wind farm through his company, Mesa Power. When completed, it will be capable of powering one million homes. That equals a lot of jobs—somebody has to build, install, and maintain all of those turbines. Pickens is also raising the standard of living for local farmers by paying a $10,000 to $20,000 annual royalty for every turbine they allow on their land. To tap into these wind energy jobs, visit the website of the American Wind Energy Association (Awea.org) and search the continually updated jobs database.

GO CORPORATE
As you've read throughout this book, whether it's at Wal-Mart, Sam's Club, Home Depot, Target, J.C. Penney, or Staples, eco-aware

products are continually hitting store shelves. Consumers are demanding green products, and the largest corporations on this planet are responding. As a result, opportunities are increasing for green-minded corporate professionals with backgrounds in finance, operations, human resources, design, marketing, and brand management.

Take Clorox. In January 2008, the company introduced a new line of natural cleaning products called Green Works. Made from 99 percent plant-based, biodegradable materials, the brand is an affordable, widely accessible, healthy solution for cleaning the home. By Earth Day 2008, it was already the market leader in its natural product categories—such as all-purpose, bathroom, toilet bowl, and glass and surface cleaners. This is good news for consumers and great news for everyone who works for the Green Works brand. From operations professionals responsible for making sure Green Works products reach retail stores to marketers who generate awareness of the brand and accountants who tally up sales, employees of this Clorox division are being paid to foster positive environmental change.

One way to identify large companies that are spearheading environmental initiatives is through Climate Counts, a nonprofit organization that ranks businesses according to environmental criteria that are sifted into four main categories: 1) measuring climate footprint; 2) actively reducing impact on global warming; 3) publicly disclosing this environmental information; and 4) supporting progressive climate legislation. Companies ranking at or near the top on these measures include Nike, News Corporation, and General Electric. The project was developed by Stonyfield Farm founder and CEO Gary Hirshberg, who serves as chairman of the board. Through green initiatives such as purchasing organic ingredients from hundreds of local family farms to installing solar panels on its production facility to implementing company-wide reuse and recycling programs, this pioneer of organic yogurt also ranks well on the Climate Counts criteria.

Some members of the environmental community are understandably uneasy about the corporate world's recent environmental initiatives. Though it may seem counterintuitive to embrace businesses that were once accused of perpetuating a fossil-fuel based, toxic economy (serving the corporate bottom line at the expense of human and planetary health), solving the enormous environmental challenges confronting humanity requires everyone to work together. This means corporations, governments, nongovernment organizations, communities, and individuals all moving toward positive environmental change. If we can all become more comfortable with environmental shades of gray and engage corporations by applauding their environmental progress while still holding them accountable for their missteps, then we can continue to move constructively toward change and away from distrust and animosity. We won't solve environmental challenges unless the most powerful organizations, i.e., the biggest companies, contribute solutions. Divided we all lose, but together we can create a better future.

FOLLOW THE VENTURE CAPITAL

Not the corporate type? There are still plenty of options and strategies for landing your dream green job. The first order of business is to follow the money. For the past few years, venture capitalists have been pouring capital into young, green-minded companies to help them grow. Flush with cash, these young startups are often hiring and are prime places to inquire about jobs. In 2008, RecycleBank, a company that makes it easy and rewarding to recycle, raised $30 million to expand its services throughout the United States. eSolar, a company that plans to build solar power plants starting in Southern California, raised $130 million. And Gridpoint, a company that helps make the energy grid more efficient, raised $15 million in addition to the more than $100 million it's raised since launching in 2003. From entry- to executive-level jobs, you can be sure these companies and others like them are staffing up. Take eSolar, which was founded in 2007 and one year later already had 70 employees. The pace of investment is quickening too. In the first six months of 2008, venture capitalists invested more than $700 million in solar energy companies—the same amount that was invested in solar for all of 2007. To track these venture capital investments, visit regularly updated blogs such as Earth2tech.com and Greenvc.org. Also check out CNET's Green Tech blog (Cnet. com/greentech) and click on "Deals and Investments."

PROMOTE CHANGE FROM WITHIN

Sometimes the best way to get a green job is to remain exactly where you are and let green opportunities come to you. A few short years ago, it was common thinking that most corporations were too entrenched in traditional ways of doing business to embrace substantive environmental change. This no longer holds true. Today companies in nearly every industry—whether it's Exxon Mobil in energy, MTV Networks in media, or Dell Computers in computer electronics—are assessing how they do business and implementing environmental measures directly into their day-to-day operations. For Exxon Mobil this means investing nearly half a billion dollars in a new factory that will manufacture a key battery component for next-generation hybrid cars running on lithium-ion batteries. At MTV Networks, the Kids and Family Division prints *Nickelodeon Magazine* on 100 percent recycled paper and creates environmental messages for youth through innovative strategies like multiplayer online eco-themed games. And Dell Computers uses energy-efficient software in its employee computers to better manage energy costs and reduce greenhouse gas emissions. Odds are your own company is rolling out some kind of green initiative. Now's the time to get involved. To learn about green initiatives inside your company, ask your boss and also check to see what information is available on your company's intranet. If that doesn't yield results, do an Internet search. See if you can identify news articles referencing people at your company working on sustainability programs. Go talk to those people, express your interest, and see how to get involved. Initially this may require you to volunteer on a green task force or committee. Do it. Even if it doesn't lead to an immediate green career opportunity, you'll build your network and position yourself for future openings.

RESEARCH NEW OPENINGS

When there are no green openings at your current company, don't despair. There are plenty of online green job boards that will help you search for a good fit someplace else. Greenjobsearch. org enables you to search by keywords or location to identify a broad range of opportunities. The more specifics you give—using terms like "solar manager" or "wind turbine installer"—the more relevant the results will be. Greenjobs.com focuses specifically on jobs available in the renewable energy industries, while the Green Dream Jobs section of SustainableBusiness.com is a great resource for short- and long-term positions with green companies and non-profit organizations. Check out the job board at Treehugger. com, one of the web's largest environmental sites, for a tremendous array of current job openings all over the United States and Greenbiz.com's Green Careers section for high-quality openings at many of today's brightest green companies and organizations. A quick scan reveals job openings for positions such as "Senior Energy Associate" at the nonprofit Sierra Club or "Sustainability Researcher" at Perkins+Will, one of the leading sustainable architecture firms in the country.

NETWORK YOUR WAY TO A GREEN GIG

Across the country, green networking groups are taking up bar space at some of the swankiest spots in town. An excellent way to learn about green job opportunities in your area is to join them. Perhaps the largest environmental networking group is Green Drinks International. Every month in cities across the United States and overseas, working professionals, students, and green-minded people of all persuasions and political affiliations, gather to toast in the name of the planet. New York City's Green Drinks chapter is in a class of its own. Founder Margaret Lydecker has built one of the most popular roving monthly events in the city. Attendance has grown from about 50 to 60 people three or fours years ago to upward of 400 people each month. The party goes particularly off-the-hook during the holidays, when close to 1,000 people are routinely on hand to get their green groove on, meet other folks with like-minded interests, and discover new opportunities for green career advancement.

For entrepreneurs and business professionals, sustainable business networks are increasingly cropping up in cities and states around the country. Many are founded with the goal of building thriving sustainable local economies and communities. Members often seek ways to collaborate and enhance each other's businesses. Most of the organizations also belong to BALLE (Business Alliance for Local Living Economies), an organization based in the United States and Canada, that connects local business networks with the goal of creating a sustainable global economy consisting of healthy local economies. This dynamic movement is attracting many green business leaders.

Net Impact is another top-notch organization dedicated to promoting positive social and environmental change through business. The first chapters were originally started at business schools throughout the United States. The organization has since expanded to include other graduate programs and professional chapters. Local chapters typically hold monthly networking and informational events where green professionals are invited to share their experience and expertise. The Net Impact annual national conference is a truly inspiring event drawing hundreds of students and green business leaders from around the world.

DON'T FORGET TO BLOG

As many business pundits have noted, each of us (whether we like it or not) is a brand. In the eyes of the world—that is, the eyes of your bosses, professors, peers, co-workers, committee members, teammates, and so on—you stand for something. You are the brand "You." And an excellent way to create green job opportunities for yourself is to green your brand. The easiest and most effective way to build and manage your brand is to create your own blog. Free software from sites like Wordpress.org or Blogger.com makes it simple and affordable to get started. On your blog you can write about green topics, load audio podcasts, and show green videos that you've made. Blogging is a great way to demonstrate your green interests and expertise. Content you post to your blog is indexed by search engines like Google, so when reporters, recruiters, entrepreneurs, or other like-minded people do searches for subjects you've written about, you stand a good chance of being found.

Before the *Lazy Environmentalist* was a national radio show, book series, or even its own branded blog, it was the title of a simple post that I wrote for my blog on Vivavi.com (the website for my green furniture company). Below is the original Lazy Environmentalist entry that I posted on January 5, 2005. A radio producer found it—and me—through a Google search and offered me the opportunity to host my own radio show. Before I knew it, one green opportunity had led to the next. Here's the entry:

January 5, 2005

Lazy Environmentalist

I'm a passionate yet lazy environmentalist. I want to do the right thing. I want the planet to be clean. I want to breathe fresh air. I want to not have to hold my breath every time I drive on the New Jersey Turnpike.

I want it to be totally fun, cool, and sexy to act in an environmentally responsible way. Otherwise, half the time I won't do it. I won't always place my empty water bottles in the recycling bin. Why? Because, frankly, it's a pain and there's nothing fun about it.

I want a shower that cleans, filters, and reuses the same five gallons of water repeatedly so I can take a low-impact 30-minute shower and know that I'm not squandering our dwindling supply of fresh water. Frankly, I take long showers. That's where I do my best thinking. So I want someone to invent this kind of shower for me. I'll be thrilled to buy it, and I'll tell all my friends to get one too.

Give me a hybrid Audi TT so I can put the top down and drive fast without polluting like a maniac. I'll gladly pay for it. Make

*me furniture out of bamboo instead of wood so I'm not by exten-
sion cutting down trees just to have something nice to eat on. I'll
pay for that too.*

*Make it so totally easy, fun, and attractive to do "the right thing"
and I'll do it every time. Because I care about the planet. I really
do. But I'm lazy, and I'm not going to change my behavior any
time soon. So cater to me. Help me consume more responsibly
without having to try. I'll thank you for it, and the planet will
too.*

When looking for a green job, your blog may connect you to
a potential employer. If your goal is to collaborate with others on
green projects, your blog can help people learn about your perspective and insights. As I've learned, blogging is an essential tool
that can lead to unexpected career-expanding opportunities. I still
regularly update my own blog at Lazyenvironmentalist.com. Come
visit.

Organizations

AMERICAN WIND ENERGY ASSOCIATION
Awea.org
The trade association for wind energy, the AWEA maintains an extensive job
board for those looking for opportunities within the industry. Job positions
span the gamut of expertise from finance to operations to construction and
quality control. Major industry players like GE, BP, and Vestas list job openings here.

BUSINESS ALLIANCE FOR LOCAL LIVING ECONOMIES (BALLE)
Livingeconomies.org
An organization based in the United States and Canada that creates and
strengthens local economies. More than 15,000 sustainable entrepreneurs
belong to BALLE through membership in their local sustainable business networks. Visit the site to learn more about the movement and find a local
sustainable business network near you.

CLIMATE COUNTS
Climatecounts.org
A nonprofit organization that ranks businesses according to environmental criteria that are sifted into four main categories: 1) measuring climate footprint; 2) actively reducing impact on global warming; 3) publicly disclosing this environmental information; and 4) supporting progressive climate legislation. It's a useful tool to focus your green job search on large companies that are spearheading environmental initiatives.

ECOBROKER INTERNATIONAL
Ecobroker.com
Licensed real estate agents can boost their eco-credentials by becoming a certified Ecobroker. Ecobroker International equips professionals with the knowledge to advise both residential and commercial clients on the environmental merits of every type of building, from houses and apartments to office parks and manufacturing facilities. More than 3,000 real estate agents throughout the United States have already been certified.

GREEN COLLAR VETS
Greencollarvets.com
Dallas-based green building entrepreneur Jyl Dehaven started Green Collar Vets, a nonprofit organization that steers military veterans toward green job opportunities. Veterans receive training in high-growth green building-related industries learning to install everything from solar panels to natural wall plasters.

GREEN DRINKS INTERNATIONAL
Biothinking.com / greendrinks
Every month in cities across the United States and around the world, environmental professionals, students, and people who are simply interested in positive environmental change gather over cocktails to network and learn about new opportunities emerging in the green economy. The more you go, the more green friends you'll make too.

GREEN FOR ALL
Greenforall.org
Green for All is an organization dedicated to building a broad coalition of support for green collar jobs. In 2007, it was instrumental in pressing Congress to pass the Green Jobs Act, which authorized $125 million per year to create a federal Energy Efficiency and Renewable Energy Worker Training Program. Green collar jobs include retrofitting buildings for energy efficiency, installing solar panels and green roofs, building wind farms, and refining waste oil into biodiesel.

NATIONAL ALTERNATIVE FUELS TRAINING CONSORTIUM

Naftc.wvu.edu

Headquartered at West Virginia University, the NAFTC conducts workshops and develops curriculums in alternative fuels, alternative fuel vehicles, and advanced technologies for its educational institution members located throughout the United States. More than 7,500 technicians have been trained to handle the nation's emerging fleets of alternative fuel vehicles. Visit the site to find a program near you. Technicians trained to maintain alternative fuel vehicles are in high demand.

NET IMPACT

Netimpact.org

Net impact is an organization dedicated to promoting positive social and environmental change through business. Chapters can be found at most business schools throughout the country and many overseas too. Local professional chapters provide an excellent means to meet people who can point you toward green career opportunities. Chapters typically meet monthly and also invite green speakers to share their experience and expertise.

U.S. GREEN BUILDING COUNCIL

Usgbc.org

The driving force behind today's green building boom, the USGBC has established its LEED (Leadership in Environmental and Energy Design) certification as the most widely adopted green building standard covering all types of buildings, from office towers to single-family homes. LEED accreditation is typically sought by real estate developers, architects, interior designers, engineers, contractors, product manufacturers and suppliers, and consultants who advise on the development of green building projects. If you're looking to break into the green building industry, obtaining LEED accreditation can jump-start your career.

Jobs Search Sites

GREENBIZ.COM

Check out the Green Careers of Greenbiz.com to find job openings at many of the brightest green companies and organizations. A quick scan reveals job openings for positions such as "Senior Energy Associate" at the nonprofit Sierra Club or "Sustainability Researcher" at Perkins+Will, one of the leading sustainable architecture firms in the United States. Job openings are being added on a daily basis.

GREENJOBS.COM
Greenjobs.com focuses specifically on jobs available in the renewable energy industries and is particularly strong for science and engineering types.

GREENJOBSEARCH.ORG
Use this website's search function to identify a broad range of opportunities listed on job board sites across the Internet. The more narrowly you define your search, the more relevant the results will be. Enter terms like "solar manager" or "wind turbine installer" to find available openings.

SUSTAINABLEBUSINESS.COM
The Green Dream Jobs section of this website is a great resource for short- and long-term positions with green companies and nonprofit organizations. Jobs are available at all levels from entry- to mid- to senior-level positions.

TREEHUGGER.COM
One of the Internet's largest environmental websites, Treehugger.com boats an impressive green jobs board. You can search by "what" or "where" to hone in on specific opportunities and set up customized job alert email notifications so you can be the first to know and the first to apply.

Information/Education

75 GREEN BUSINESSES
75greenbusinesses.com
Pick up a copy of this book by Glen Croston to learn about emerging careers and business opportunities throughout the green economy. In each chapter, Croston provides lots of background information and points you toward specific careers like running a green bed and breakfast, making green furniture, or installing solar panels.

CAREERS IN RENEWABLE ENERGY: GET A GREEN ENERGY JOB
Pixyjackpress.com
Published in 2008, this book tells you everything you need to know to plan for a career in the field of renewable energy. Learn which courses to take, certifications to obtain, associations to belong to, and industries to target in order to successfully launch your career. Author Gregory McNamee also provides plenty of background information on renewable energy technologies like solar, wind, geothermal, and hydrogen.

CNET

Cnet.com/greentech

CNET is a top online destination for technology news, and its coverage of green developments does not disappoint. Visit the Green Tech blog and click on "Deals and Investments" to discover companies that are receiving millions of dollars in venture capital investment. Young companies flush with cash make good targets for green job hunters. Check it out.

EARTH2TECH.COM

Track the latest developments in the world of green technology at this continually updated blog. Earth2tech.com also features a map of 101 "cleantech" startups—the companies on the front lines of the renewable energy revolution. Check it out, read up on the players, and contact them to see whether you can tie your career prospects and salary to building a clean energy future.

GREENVC.ORG

A website devoted to tracking venture capital investment in young green companies, Greenvc.org helps you discover electric car companies, green building products companies, and solar energy companies that are receiving millions of dollars to grow their businesses. Most businesses need to hire people in order to grow. Now's the time to send your resume.

THE LAZY ENVIRONMENTALIST

Lazyenvironmentalist.com/jobs

I've created a special page to keep Lazy Environmentalist readers updated about ongoing developments in the world of green employment. Stay on top of emerging trends that could land you in your green dream job.

ACKNOWLEDGMENTS

I wish to thank my Lazy Environmentalist compadres Margaret Teich, Jodi Fontana, and Aron Kressner who make for great traveling companions as we explore ways to make environmentalism resonate with the great majority. To Marisa Belger, thank you for applying your marvelous editing skills to this project and helping me to once again find and stay true to "my voice." To my editor, Dervla Kelly, thank you for so artfully giving this project the breathing room to come to life. To my book agent, Mel Parker, thank you for being both a true friend and a trusted advisor. To Sarah Beatty, founder of Green Depot, thank you for patiently explaining the sometimes arcane details of green building products. To Elka Boren, the best shaman a man could have, thank you for continuing to align my chakras so I can think straighter. To Herb "The Godfather" Sydney, thank you for remaining ceaselessly in my corner and bestowing your wonderful advice. To Bill and Jancy Dorfman, thank you for being such cool parents and for trusting me with the keys to your sweet home in Asheville, North Carolina where I wrote much of this book. To my brother and sister in-law, Jed and Carolyn Dorfman, thank you for your extremely (I mean, extremely) honest feedback about the book's contents and for implementing many of these eco-ideas at Camp Walt Whitman, the children's sleep-away camp which has been run by members of my family for over 60 years. Finally, to the legions of green entrepreneurs and innovators, thank you for continuing to do the heavy eco-lifting so that my baby niece, Addie, and those of her generation may never have to.

Did you know Americans send 38

billion water bottles a year to landfills?[1] If laid end to end, that's enough bottles to travel from the Earth to the Moon and back 10 times.[2] If placed in a landfill or littered, those bottles could take up to 1,000 years to biodegrade.[3]

Join Josh Dorfman and make a difference by supporting the FilterForGood campaign. Brita and Nalgene teamed up to create FilterForGood, a campaign committed to reducing bottled water waste by filling a reusable bottle with filtered tap water. Visit www. filterforgood.com to learn more, purchase a FilterForGood bottle made by Nalgene and take the FilterForGood Pledge. To help you keep your commitment, print a coupon for $5 off a Brita system or $1 off a filter after you pledge.

FILTERFORGOOD.COM℠

MADE IN USA

---

1 Fishman, Charles. "Message in a Bottle." *Fast Company Magazine* July 2007: 110.

2 All distance statistics are calculated by dividing a known length by .67 feet (or 8 inches, the height of an average water bottle), e.g., Route 66 is 2,400 miles or 12,672,000 feet, and Americans use 955.8 million bottles a week, which would stretch more than 637 million feet if laid end-to-end. The distance those bottles would cover divided by the length of Route 66 is equal to 50.28, meaning the bottles could travel Route 66 more than 50 times.

3 Arnold, Emily, and Janet Larsen. "Bottled Water: Pouring Resources Down the Drain." *Earth Policy Institute.* 2 Feb. 2006. 28 June 2007 (http://www.earthpolicy.org/Updates/2006/Update51.htm).